THE JOLLY BEGGARS

OR

LOVE & LIBERTY

A Cantata.

THE JOLLY BEGGARS

OR

LOVE & LIBERTY

by

ROBERT BURNS

With A Facsimile Of a Hand-Written Copy Prepared By The Poet Himself.

LUATH PRESS
Barr, Ayrshire.

First Edition 1984

ISBN 0 946487 02 2

CONTENTS

INTRODUCTION

Love and Liberty or *The Jolly Beggars* was a unique effort by Robert Burns. He did nothing similar to it ever again, and indeed, if he is to be believed, thought so little of it that he forgot its very existence. And yet it is surely one of the finest flowerings of his poetic genius.

The Cantata — for that is how Burns described it — records a Beggars' Revel in a low dive at Mauchline, near where Burns lived. Quite a number of vagabonds were at that carousal, and Burns gives songs to six of them — a sodger and his drab, a Merry Andrew or fool, a pickpocket carlin, a little fiddler, and the caird or tinker. Others were mentioned, but given no song — the Merry Andrew's Grizzie and the Fiddler's Twa Deborahs. And of course the Poet or Bard himself has two songs, the best of all.

The Jolly Beggars is not the only 'one-off' job Burns wrote. *Tam O' Shanter* was also a unique effort, and a work of equal genius. Never a Burns Nicht Supper passes without some reference to what might have been written if Burns had lived longer. And, trite though it may be, that is a perfectly proper thought. He wrote but one *Tam O' Shanter*, a Tale told in verse of great genius, and yet he had a hundred more similar old Scots tales in his head, ready to write down. Indeed, he had no less than three distinct versions of the *Tam O' Shanter* tale itself. He wrote but one such work as *The Jolly Beggars* (which incidentally would be much better titled *Love and Liberty* as Burns probably intended — this present manuscript calls it only *A Cantata,* but another one is known to have had the title of *Love and Liberty, a Cantata*). And although he wrote but one such, his mind was full of stories from Scottish history and fable, and he regretted that no one was mining that great seam for the stage. He wrote:-

1

There's themes enow in Caledonian story
Would show the Tragic Muse in all her glory.—
Is there no daring Bard will rise and tell
How glorious Wallace stood, how hapless fell?
Where are the Muses fled that could produce
A drama worthy o' the name o' Bruce?

We can never know for sure, but very possibly he was himself thinking of such writing for the stage. And of more Tales in verse, like *Tam O' Shanter*. And perhaps even of more such works as *The Jolly Beggars*. The possibilities were multitude but they all ended miserably with his early death. A tragedy indeed, and a sad loss that such a multi-faceted genius should die so young.

It is very odd that *The Jolly Beggars* should be so little known and so rarely performed, even in Scotland. And yet when it has been performed, the reception was rapturous. One wonders why our National Opera Company should not produce it as an intermezzo between the acts of some opera, a practice once popular but now forgotten. Its vigour, truth, and earthiness would be a grand refreshment between the acts of many an operatic evening.

Or, indeed, perhaps, why not drop *Cavalleria Rusticana* from the time-worn 'Cav. and Pag.', and play *The Jolly Beggars* instead? *Pagliacci* and *The Jolly Beggars* would surely provide an evening of pure magic.

It is now thirty years since *The Jolly Beggars* has had much exposure. In 1953, Cedric Thorpe Davie produced a chamber version for four voices and an instrumental ensemble for the Braemar Music Festival. This was later staged at the Edinburgh Festival, televised, broadcast and recorded. It was a grand production, especially in the version played by the Saltire Music Group, and was very popular throughout Scotland, even when seen on the tiny, flickering black-and-white screens of the day. The time has surely come, though, for a revival. There is a new generation which has not even had the opportunity of seeing and hearing one of Scotland's cultural glories.

The cantata form was well established — a recitativo bringing on the first character and his song. Then recitativo, then song, to the end. Inevitably, Burns did not follow that precise pattern, but varied it, giving the Poet two songs, including the spectacular Finale. But then, everything about *The Jolly Beggars* is variety and change — variety as complex and manifold as the beggars themselves. The metres he uses, the very language he deploys, all serve to establish the atmosphere of the Beggars Revel. His use of language to establish atmosphere was ever one of Burns's many aspects of genius. Recall how the quietness and simplicity of *The Cottar* is established in the first few lines, just by the genius of the words chosen. In *The Jolly Beggars,* by his metrical variety and superb skill with words, Burns demonstrated for all time his complete mastery of his trade.

The more one reads *The Jolly Beggars*, the more some very puzzling questions come to mind. Why, for example, are most of the songs in English, and the *recitativos* in good Scots? Those *recitativos* are great vernacular poetry, and they frame and bring to life the singers themselves, and this is necessary because the songs, generally, are somewhat flat. But that does not apply to the Poet's Songs, and here one presumes that the Poet was Burns himself.

Even more puzzling is the question why Burns thought so little of this whole work that he claimed to have forgotten all about it, and to have only the vaguest recollections of one song (The Poet's Finale) which had somewhat pleased him.

Even when it was finally published, *The Jolly Beggars* was by no means well appreciated in all of Scotland. Glasgow and the south-west of the country immediately fell under the spell of its magic — strolling vagabonds were still a common-place of life there. Edinburgh, especially the *literati*, showed no understanding or appreciation of it, and in the Highlands, where strolling vagabonds were few, there was no understanding at all.

The most prominent writers of the Lowlands were unanimous in their praise, although Carlyle thought that the subject matter was 'the lowest in nature.' One must wonder how much Carlyle knew of the low life, and how much he understood of what little he did know. Just the same, Carlyle thought *The Jolly Beggars* the most poetic of Burns's pieces.

Of course, Burns did in fact write often, and brilliantly, of those things which the socially fastidious would consider 'low'. The mouse, the louse, a daisy, Holy Willie, are hardly subjects which the poetic of his day would consider suitable subjects. One prominent aesthete had but recently pronounced that the only subjects fit for poetry were love and wine! Not for Burns, though, the glory of the rose, but rather the simplicity of the daisy; not the emaciated loves of Princes, but the faithfulness of John Anderson and the beauty of the Lass o' Ballochmyle; not the attainments of Generals but the fornications of Holy Willie. Although he lived amidst the glorious scenery of South-west Scotland, he wrote hardly a word of description of it. It cannot have been that he, with his fine sensibilities, failed to appreciate it (although, in truth, appreciation of the beauty of one's surroundings is partly a function of affluence and leisure.) Rather he chose to write of the things which his friends and neighbours would appreciate, and what they had themselves observed. They would most certainly have seen the sun descend in glory over Arran at the close of a winter's day, but it was more important to get the weary and steaming horse unyoked from the plough and turn homewards than spend time watching the colours change in the sunset. In his choice of subjects, Burns long predated the English Lake Poets, who believed all subjects were fit for poetic treatment. And they were the poetic revolutionaries of their day.

It was Sir Walter Scott, with his own rather surprising understanding of the vagabonds' life, who most praised *The Jolly Beggars,* and showed a profound sympathy with it. He strongly criticised the editor who omitted it from The Collected Works.

Outside Scotland, Mathew Arnold, who had himself written *The Scholar Gypsy*, described *The Jolly Beggars* as 'this puissant and splendid production'. The Editors of The Centenary Edition referred to it as 'this irresistible presentation of humanity caught in the act, and summarised for ever in terms of art'. Angellier, the great French writer on Burns, thought that *The Jolly Beggars* was Burns's masterpiece, not that it was necessarily his greatest work, but in the proper sense of 'masterpiece' in which a craftsman demonstrates his total mastery of his craft.

And yet Burns claimed to have forgotten this masterpiece!

The Jolly Beggars was written towards the end of 1785, when, at the age of 26, Burns was having a particularly difficult time. His father had died at Lochlea the previous year, and the family, with Robert as the head, had moved to a new small farm at Mossgiel, near Mauchline. Burns was sorely troubled by his father's death, and as always happens when those we love die, was beset by notions of sins of omission and commission. He had firmly resolved to lead a life of sobriety and uprightness, to accept his many new responsibilities, and to settle down and be a good farmer.

In fact, he did all of those things, and firmly settled his neck into the collar of very hard work. And indeed, for a small farmer on that land in those days, it *was* hard work.

But he was not just a farmer — he was Robert Burns the poet. His genius could not be contained within the bounds of a small farm, even though he drew much inspiration from that small farm, and much wonderful poetry flowed from it. He did indeed try to bow his neck to the yoke, but he was young, he was a poet, he was Robert Burns, and the blood tingled in his veins.

Before long he was spending evenings in Mauchline. Not those evenings of heavy drinking and whoring that later legend attributed to him, but a good deal of talk and comradeship — and a few drinks — in the local taverns. They were good evenings, spent with good friends, and in no way did they interfere with his farming, for he remained determined to fulfil all the obligations he had undertaken as head of his family.

Amongst his friends were John Richmond and James Smith. Richmond was clerk to the solicitor Gavin Hamilton, who was Burns's landlord at Mossgiel, and Richmond long remained one of Burns's closest friends. James Smith, another boon companion, kept a small draper's shop in Mauchline. The two of them, like Burns himself, eventually found Mauchline too small and confining. Richmond went to Edinburgh, and Smith to Jamaica. He died at St. Lucia.

Burns directed one of his fine *Epistles* to James Smith, and in it he wrote freely of his views on poetry and on life. It sheds a great deal of light on those years when the poet, while working deathly hard on an unproductive farm, grew and matured in his genius. His deep affection for James Smith shines through that remarkable *Epistle:-*

> *Then, Jamie, I shall say nae mair,*
> *But quat my song.*
> *Content wi' you to make a pair*
> *Where'er I gang.*

Burns, Richmond and Smith were the three members of The Court Of Equity, a very elaborate joke in verse, supposed to be a Court sitting in judgement on local fornicators, and protecting the welfare of the local girls. The three — they called themselves Fornicators By Profession — were in a good position to know the gossip and scandal of the village (indeed, they themselves provoked much of it!), and Burns's ready pen set it down in delightful, bawdy language. Not surprisingly, he was again in trouble with the Kirk Session as a result of The Court Of Equity. It seemed that he had not been sufficiently chastened after the episode of Holy Willie's Prayer.

It is supposed that one Mauchline night, the three were in a local tavern when they heard that there was a beggars' revel taking place in Poosie Nansie's, close by. Poosie Nansie Gibson kept a dive in the village, a place of bad reputation, a sort of lodging house and drinking place for the many vagrants and beggars who travelled the Scottish Lowlands in those days, living as they could and sleeping rough in such places as Poosie Nansie's. Poosie Nansie had a daughter, Racer Jess, who served in the tavern, and was one of the local whores. Her nickname 'Racer' came from her practice of running wherever she went.

It seems that the three of them (or possibly only two of them) went to Poosie Nansie's to see the fun. Only, for Burns at least, it was not all fun. He found himself deeply affected by what he saw and heard that night.

The beggars and vagrants, men and women, seemed to have a joy in life, and a liberty, that other, more settled folk, though richer, had never even glimpsed. Here were those whom a heartless society had rejected, and those who did not fit into the moulds required by that society. And they did not care. Largely, they had chosen their way of life, and consequently they had liberty of a curious kind, liberty from the bonds and boundaries imposed by society. They had liberty to live and love as they chose, even if that liberty and that love could be exercised only in hedge-rows and barns and in such dives as that of Poosie Nansie.

One can well understand how this would appeal to Burns. He was smarting under the whip with which that peculiar society of his day sought to regulate the actions — even the thoughts — of all its members. He was struggling at Mossgeil against physical and economic problems that seemed to increase day by day. He was a natural rebel anyway, but also a poet, one whose very mind and being responded to the unusual, the bizarre, the rebellious.

It was the task of the poet, he saw, to interprete that love and liberty to all the rest of society, to put into words the inchoate emotions aroused in him by what he saw and heard that night in Poosie Nansie's.

This he did, in a work of great power and feeling.   There is no condescension in *The Jolly Beggars,* none of the bitter irony of which Burns was master.   Rather, he shows a very deep love and understanding of the people he observed with so much sympathy, of their hopes and sorrows, their fears and their joys.   It is a superlative demonstration of compassion, even, in a strange way, of envy.   With his words, Burns drew pictures of that low life as vivid as ever Rowlandson did with his pencil.   Rowlandson, not Hogarth, for in the *The Jolly Beggars* there is none of the ugliness and viciousness which Hogarth limned with his genius.   Perhaps the only comparable work in words is that scarifying picture of human aspirations amidst degradation drawn by Maxim Gorki in his *Lower Depths.*

Using old and well loved tunes for the songs, and traditional, but varied metres for the *recitativos,* Burns allowed his characters to sketch themselves and their stories. Then, in the *recitativos,* in vernacular verse of ferocious power, he ties them all together, places them in context, and brings them to life.

The 'Cantata' form was not strange to Burns, nor to Scotland. Indeed, a Scottish King, James, the Gaberlunzie Man, had himself written one.   And Ramsay also wrote one.   The 18th century loved Cantatas, and Ramsay, in his *The Merry Beggars* played that field.   Understandably, Burns knew these works, but he did not, being Robert Burns, follow their pattern.   Ramsay's beggars are but cardboard figures — a poet, a lawyer, a soldier, a courtier, a fiddler and a preacher.   Hardly the sort of people to be found tramping the long Scottish roads.

Those long Scottish roads, at least in the Lowlands, swarmed with beggars in the 18th century. They were licensed to beg, and to carry a wallet for their takings. Edie Ochiltree, as Sir Walter Scott described her, wore an official beggar's blue gown and a badge, and Sir Walter, incidentally, seemed to know well the life on the roads.   Madge Wildfire, in *The Heart of Midlothian*, is a very vivid picture of a beggar woman. One wonders how Scott, so bound to his books and his desk, learned so much of them. The licensed beggars were a multitude — old soldiers, tinkers, old women, refugees from the Highlands, farm workers dispossessed by new farming methods, widows and orphans — a great host of displaced persons, living as best they could and making the best of a bad job.

The beggars brought to life by Burns certainly seemed to have no regrets about their lives. They seemed to love the roads, and have no intention of leaving them. Unlike King James's *And we'll gang nae mair a-roving, a-roving, a-roving in the night* or Byron's *We'll go no more a roving by the light of the moon*, the vagabonds revelling in Poosie Nansie's seemed content with their lot, and determined to keep on roving, enjoying their peculiar liberties and loves.

Of course, Burns, with the poetical eye of his genius, knew them all. *The Jolly Beggars* was certainly no sudden flash of inspiration. Indeed, little of his work was, even if the actual composition was quick and seemed easy. Burns was a close observer, and most of his work was the result of a slow germination and a steady growth, culminating in the flowers of poetry he left us. Always, he wrote from intimate knowledge. All his life he had observed the Holy Willies, the Cottars, the Beggars, as well as the mice and the lice. When the time came for his understanding of these things to be written, his genius was able to draw on long and profound observation.

Very sadly, some of the songs, and therefore presumably some of the *recitativos,* have disappeared from extant copies of *The Jolly Beggars*. John Richmond spoke later of songs by a sweep, a sailor and by Racer Jess herself, but these prunings (and whose hand did the pruning?) are no longer known. We cannot now know why *The Jolly Beggars* did not appear in the Kilmarnock Edition, Burns's first printed book, but it seems that he wished to include it in the Edinburgh Edition, which followed shortly afterwards. However, the Rev. Hugh Blair, one of the self-appointed arbiters of 'good taste' who so sadly influenced Burns, advised against it, and it was not included. A pity.

It was first published in Glasgow in 1799, although there had been interest in it before the poet's death. Oddly, as early as 1793, Burns wrote, in response to enquiries from

George Thompson (Editor of *A Select Edition of Original Scottish Airs,* and a good friend of Burns) that he had forgotten about *The Jolly Beggars,* and that he had kept no copy. He remembered that none of the songs pleased him, except the Finale:-

> *Courts for Cowards were erected,*
> *Churches built to please the Priest.*

Fortunately, Burns had the good practice of making several copies of his works, and distributing them to his friends, for their delight and criticism. It would be very natural that James Smith and John Richmond received copies of *The Jolly Beggars,* since they were so intimately concerned with it, and the copy in Burns's own handwriting, of which this book is a facsimile, is claimed to have been given by Burns to David Woodburn, factor to Mr. Adam of Craigingillan. Interestingly, the sweep's song, and the others now lost, are missing from this manuscript copy; clearly they were pruned at a very early date.

Critically speaking, this great work of a master poet is flawed, as all man-made artifacts are flawed somewhere. The songs, most of them, do not have the vigour, realism and vulgarity that would have befitted the occasion. Most of them are rather out of character, and, even stranger, are in English, with only the Fiddler's Song having a little of the Scots tongue. And yet they are all brought into sharp focus and contrast by the strength and vigour of those oddly entitled *recitativos.* Those are in verse vernacular, sharp, brief and of quite remarkable power. It may well be that Burns, experimenting as always with the languages and the verse forms he so loved, quite deliberately sought this contrast, and used it to sharpen the effect of the whole.

Whatever the reality, the fact is that he seems to have been dissatisfied with the final results. But although the artist is always ultimately the best judge of his own work, Burns was in a strange position. He was a young man, living in remote villages, little touched by the intellectual and artistic ferment of the capital city, and, understandably, rather in awe of those *literati* who fussed around the edges of that ferment. He was a genius, but a genius in transition and growth, and although it was all very well to receive the unmitigated praise of cronies like Richmond and Smith, nevertheless he must have wondered how the wider world would receive him.

In his powerful *First Epistle to John Lapraik,* Burns argues that:-

> I am nae poet, in a sense,
> But just a rhymer, like by chance,
> An' hae to learning nae pretence..........
>
> A set o' dull conceited hashes
> Confuse their brains wi' college classes,
> They gang in stirks, and come out asses,
>   Plain truth to speak,
> An' syne they think to climb Parnassus
>   By dint o' Greek............
>
> Give me ae spark o' Nature's fire,
> That's a' the learning I desire............

Is there, perhaps, a smack of sour grapes about this? Did Burns secretly consider himself somehow inferior to the college-bred asses? Certainly he later did quite a bit of kow-towing to them (who in fact had not a tithe of his intelligence and not a fraction of his skills). He listened to them, instead of to his own beautifully sharpened genius. Even much later, when his self-confidence should have been heightened, he listened to literary tapeworms who advised him, on grounds of 'good taste', to drop some vivid couplets from *Tam O' Shanter.* He listened to those who advised him, certainly knowing nothing of the Lowland Scots tongue, to change 'Stinchar' for 'Lugar' (the names of two rivers) in his delightful *'My Nanie, O',* thus making a nonsense out of the descriptions, but pleasing, presumably, those who thought 'Stinchar' would be pronounced 'Stinkar'.

Perhaps this quite unfounded feeling of inferiority, this fear of offending the literary parasites, led him to put *The Jolly Beggars* to one side. (I find it quite impossible to believe that he had actually forgotten it.) However, it reappeared after his death, and we are duly grateful. But, strangely, even today it is the one major work of Burns that is still little known, and sadly neglected. Perhaps it does not fit into any particular category of poetry or song. (But neither does *Tam O' Shanter.)* Perhaps, even for today, the powerful sentiments are medicine a little too bitter.

Whatever the reasons, it is a grossly neglected work.   In praising it, there is in fact little to add to the long paean from Sir Walter Scott, printed in The Advertisement following this Introduction.   *The Jolly Beggars or Love and Liberty* is a unique expression of poetic genius: we are fortunate to have it.

Tom Atkinson

FAC-SIMILE

OF

BURNS' CELEBRATED POEM,

ENTITLED THE

JOLLY BEGGARS.

FROM THE ORIGINAL MANUSCRIPT,

IN THE POSSESSION OF

THOMAS STEWART, Esq. Greenock.

PUBLISHED BY JAMES LUMSDEN & SON, GLASGOW;
WILLIAM BLACKWOOD, EDINBURGH; AND LONGMAN & CO. LONDON.
1823.

ADVERTISEMENT.

In reading performances that we admire, we naturally feel anxious to know something of the face and figure of the author, of his habits, and of all those little peculiarities which are supposed to accompany genius. It affords, too, no inconsiderable gratification to see the hand-writing, or a fac-simile of it, of eminent men. The fac-simile of the Round Robin, in Boswell's Life of Johnson, is perhaps not the least entertaining relic among the numerous memoranda of the celebrated wits and writers of his day, which that entertaining work contains; but of all the documents of this kind, none of such length and variety as that of the Jolly Beggars, now presented to the public, was ever published, so far as we know; it contains specimens of the several varieties of Burns' hand-writing, large and small, and the accuracy with which it is executed, is attested by Mr. Thomas Stewart, to whom the original belongs. To those who have seen any of Burns' hand-writing, no attestation is necessary; the evidence it carries on its own face is sufficient.

The Manuscript was given by the Poet himself to Mr. David Woodburn, at that time factor to Mr. Adam of Craigingillan, and by Mr. Woodburn to Mr. Robert M'Limont, merchant in Glasgow, from whom it passed into the possession of Mr. Smith of Greenock, who gave it to the present possessor.

It was first printed along with some other poems in a thin octavo volume, published at Glasgow in 1801, under the title of '.Poems ascribed to Robert Burns, the Ayrshire bard.' It was afterwards set to music by Bishop, and published by Mr. George Thomson of Edinburgh, in 1818; but *here*, for the first time, it appears in its native and most interesting dress, complete. Mr. Thomson, in his work, has left out some of the most characteristic verses, perhaps from over-fastidiousness; for instance, the fourth verse of the Soldier's Song: some of the others were with propriety omitted in a work like his; but the omissions have entirely or at least in a great measure destroyed the effect of the whole. It is a picture drawn from the lowest of mankind, but done with such exquisite art, that what would in other hands have been disgusting, is here in the highest degree amusing; all that would offend good taste is thrown into shade, while both nature and character are still finely preserved: it displays perhaps more than any of his other poems, the strong native humour of Burns, and his nice discrimination of character: the picture is evidently drawn from personal observation.

This exquisite cantata was introduced to general notice by the following observations in the Quarterly Review, attributed by Mr. Cromek to Sir Walter Scott:—" Yet applauding, as we do most highly applaud, the lead-" ing principles of Dr. Currie's selection, we are aware that they sometimes " led him into fastidious and over-delicate rejection of the bard's most " spirited and happy effusions. A thin octavo, published at Glasgow in " 1801, under the title of ' Poems ascribed to Robert Burns, the Ayrshire " bard,' furnishes valuable proofs of this assertion. It contains, among a " good deal of rubbish, some of his most brilliant poetry. A cantata in

" particular, called the Jolly Beggars, for humorous description and nice
" discrimination of character, is inferior to no poem of the same length in
" the whole range of English poetry. The scene, indeed, is laid in the very
" lowest department of low life, the actors being a set of strolling vagrants,
" met to carouse and barter their rags and plunder for liquor in a hedge
" ale-house. Yet, even in describing the movements of such a group, the
" native taste of the poet has never suffered his pen to slide into any thing
" coarse or disgusting. The extravagant glee and outrageous frolic of the
" beggars are ridiculously contrasted with their maimed limbs, rags, and
" crutches; the sordid and squalid circumstances of their appearance are
" judiciously thrown into the shade. Nor is the art of the poet less con-
" spicuous in the individual figures, than in the general mass. The festive
" vagrants are distinguished from each other by personal appearance and
" character, as much as any fortuitous assembly in the higher orders of life.
" The group, it must be observed, is of Scottish character, and doubtless
" our northern brethren are more familiar with its varieties than we are:
" yet the distinctions are too well marked to escape even the South'ron.
" The most prominent persons are a maimed soldier and his female com-
" panion, a hackneyed follower of the camp, a stroller, late the consort
" of an Highland ketterer or sturdy beggar,—' but weary fa' the waefu'
" woodie!' Being now at liberty, she becomes an object of rivalry be-
" tween a ' pigmy scraper with his fiddle' and a stroling tinker. The lat-
" ter, a desperate bandit, like most of his profession, terrifies the musician
" out of the field, and is preferred by the damsel, of course. A wandering
" ballad-singer, with a brace of doxies, is last introduced upon the stage.

" Each of these mendicants sings a song in character, and such a collection
" of humorous lyrics, connected by vivid poetical description, is not, per-
" haps, to be paralleled in the English language.—The concluding ditty,
" chaunted by the ballad-singer at the request of the company, whose
" ' mirth and fun have now grown fast and furious,' and set them above all
" sublunary terrors of jails, stocks, and whipping-posts, is certainly far
" superior to any thing in the Beggars' Opera, where alone we could
" expect to find its parallel.

" We are at a loss to conceive any good reason why Dr. Currie did not
" introduce this singular and humorous cantata into his collection. It is
" true, that, in one or two passages, the muse has trespassed slightly upon
" decorum, where, in the language of Scottish song,

> " ' High kilted was she,
>
> " ' As she gaed owre the lea.'

" Something, however, is to be allowed to the nature of the subject, and
" something to the education of the poet: and if, from veneration to the
" names of Swift and Dryden, we tolerate the grossness of the one, and the
" indelicacy of the other, the respect due to that of Burns, may surely claim
" indulgence for a few light strokes of broad humour."

Mr. Warren of London, has been for some time engaged in executing
a beautiful cabinet engraving, from Allan's celebrated drawing of " the
Jolly Beggars," which is now nearly finished, and will form an appropriate
accompaniment to the present publication.

FAC-SIMILE

OF

BURNS' CELEBRATED POEM,

ENTITLED THE

JOLLY BEGGARS.

A Cantata

RECITATIVO

When lyart leaves bestrow the yird,
Or, wavering like the bauckie-bird,(x)
   Bedim cauld Boreas' blast;
When hailstanes drive wi' bitter skyte,
And infant frosts begin to bite,
   In hoary cranreuch drest;
Ae night at e'en a merry core
   O' randie, gangrel bodies
In Poosie Nansie's held the splore,
   To drink their orra duddies:
     Wi' quaffing and laughing
      They ranted an' they sang,
     Wi' jumping an' thumping,
     The vera girdle rang.

First, niest the fire, in auld red rags
Ane sat; weel braced wi' mealy bags
   And knapsack a' in order;
His doxy lay within his arm,
Wi' usquebae and blankets warm
   She blinket on her sodger:

(x)The old Scotch name for the Bat

A Cantata.—

Recitativo

When lyart leaves bestrow the yird,
Or wavering like the *Bauckie-bird,
    Bedim cauld Boreas' blast;
When hailstanes drive wi' bitter skyte,
And infant Frosts begin to bite,
    In hoary cranreuch drest;
Ae night at e'en a merry core
    O' randie, gangrel bodies,
In Poosie-Nansie's held the splore,
    To drink their orra duddies:
      Wi' quaffing, and laughing,
        They ranted an' they sang;
      Wi' jumping, an' thumping,
        The vera girdle rang.

First, niest the fire, in auld, red rags,
Ane sat; weel brac'd wi' mealy bags,
    And knapsack a' in order;
His doxy lay within his arm,
Wi' usquebae an' blankets warm,
    She blinket on her Sodger:

---

* The old Scotch name for the Bat.

21

An' ay he gies the tozie drab
   The tither skelpin kiss,
While she held up her greedy gab
   Just like an aumous dish:
         Ilk smack still, did crack still,
            Just like a cadger's whip,
         Then staggering an' swaggering
            He roar'd this ditty up—

Air — Tune Soldiers joy

I am a son of Mars, who have been in many wars,
And show my cuts and scars wherever I come;
This here was for a wench, and that other in a trench
When welcoming the French at the sound of the drum.
               Lal de daudle, Etc.

My prenticeship I past, where my leader breath'd his last,
When the bloody die was cast on the heights of Abram:
And I served out my trade, when the gallant game was play'd,
And the Moro low was laid at the sound of the drum.
               Lal de daudle, Etc.

I lastly was with Curtis, among the floating batt'ries
And there I left for witness an arm and a limb;
Yet let my country need me, with Elliot to head me,
I'd clatter on my stumps at the sound of a drum.

An' ay he gies the tozie drab
    The tither skelpan kiss.
While she held up her greedy gab,
    Just like an aumous dish:
        Ilk smack still did crack still,
            Just like a cadger's whip;
        Then staggering, an' swaggering,
            He roar'd this ditty up —

Air ——— Tune Soldiers joy. —

I am a Son of Mars who have been in many wars,
    And show my cuts and scars wherever I come;
This here was for a wench, and that other in a trench,
    When welcoming the French at the sound of the drum.
                        Lal de daudle &c.

My Prenticeship I past where my Leader breath'd his last,
    When the bloody die was cast on the heights of Abram;
And I served out my Trade when the gallant Game was play'd,
    And the Moro low was laid at the sound of the drum.

I lastly was with Curtis among the floating batt'ries,
    And there I left for witness, an arm and a limb;
Yet let my Country need me, with Elliot to head me,
    I'd clatter on my stumps at the sound of a drum.

And now, tho' I must beg with a wooden arm and leg,
And many a tatter'd rag hanging over my bum,
I'm as happy with my wallet, my bottle and my callet,
As when I us'd in scarlet to follow a drum.

~~What tho', with hoary locks I must stand the winter's shocks~~
What tho', with hoary locks I must stand the winter shocks,
Beneath the woods and rocks oftentimes for a home!
When the tother bag I sell, and the tother bottle tell,
I could meet a troop of Hell at the sound of a drum!

RECITATIVO.

He ended; and the kebars sheuk
   Aboon the chorus roar;
While frightened rattons backward leuk,
   An seek the benmost bore:
A fairy fiddler frae the neuk,
   He skirl'd out, ENCORE:
But up arose the martial chuck,
   An' laid the loud uproar—

Air.   Tune.   Sodger Ladie

I once was a maid tho' I cannot tell when,
And still my delight is in proper young men;
Some one of a troop of Dragoons was my dadie;
No wonder I'm fond of a Sodger laddie.
            Sing, Lal de Lal, Etc.

And now tho' I must beg, with a wooden arm and leg,
    And many a tatter'd rag hanging over my bum,
I'm as happy with my wallet my bottle and my Callet,
    As when I us'd in scarlet to follow a drum.
~~What tho', with hoary locks, I must stand the winters shock~~
What tho', with hoary locks I must stand the winter shocks,
    Beneath the woods and rocks oftentimes for a home,
When the tother bag I sell and the tother bottle tell,
    I could meet a troop of Hell at the sound of a drum.

    Recitativo ——————

He ended; and the kebars sheuk,
    Aboon the chorus roar;
While frighted rattons backward leuk,
    An' seek the benmost bore:
A fairy Fiddler frae the neuk,
    He skirl'd out, ENCORE.
But up arose the martial Chuck,
    An' laid the loud uproar —

Air.   Tune, Sodger laddie ——————

I once was a Maid tho' I cannot tell when,
And still my delight is in proper young men:
Some one of a troop of Dragoons was my daddie,
No wonder I'm fond of a Sodger laddie.
    Sing lal de dal &c

The first of my loves was a swaggering blade;
To rattle the thundering drum was his trade;
His leg was so tight and his cheek was so ruddy,
Transported I was with my Sodger laddie.

But the godly old Chaplain left him in the lurch;
The sword I forsook for the sake of the church;
He ventur'd the soul, and I risked the Body;
'Twas then I proved false to my Sodger laddie.

Full soon I grew sick of my sanctified Sot;
The regiment at large for a husband I got;
From the gilded Spontoon to the Fife I was ready;
I asked no more but a Sodger laddie.

But the Peace it reduc'd me to beg in despair,
Till I met my old boy in a Cunningham fair;
His rags regimental they flutter'd so gaudy;
My heart it rejoic'd at a Sodger laddy.

And now I have lived—I know not how long!
And still I can join in a cup and a song;
But whilst with both hands I can hold the glass steady,
Here's to thee, my Hero, my Sodger laddie.

The first of my Loves was a swaggering blade,
To rattle the thundering drum was his trade;
His leg was so tight and his cheek was so ruddy,
Transported I was with my Sodger laddie.

But the godly old Chaplain left him in the lurch;
The sword I forsook for the sake of the church;
He ventur'd the Soul, and I risked the Body.
'Twas then I prov'd false to my Sodger laddie.

Full soon I grew sick of my sanctified Sot,
The Regiment at large for a husband I got;
From the gilded Spontoon to the Fife I was ready,
I asked no more but a Sodger laddie.

But the Peace it seduc'd me to beg in despair,
Till I met my old boy in a Cunningham fair;
His Rags regimental they flutter'd so gaudy.
My heart it rejoic'd at a Sodger laddie.

And now I have lived — I know not how long,
And still I can join in a cup and a song;
But whilst with both hands I can hold the glass steady,
Here's to thee, My Hero my Sodger laddie.

RECITATIVE.

Poor Merry andrew, in a the neuk
   Sat guzzling wi' a Tinkler-hizzie;
They mind't na wha the chorus teuk,
   Between themsels they were sae busy:
At length wi' drink an' courting dizzy,
   He stoiter'd up an' made a face;
Then turn'd an' laid a smack on Grizzie,
   Syne tun'd his pipes wi' grave grimace.

Air.   Tune, Auld Sir Symon

Sir Wisdom's a fool when he's fou;
   Sir Knave is a fool in a Session,
He's there but a prentice I trow,
But I am a fool by profession.

My Grannie she bought me a beuk,
   An' I held awa to the School;
I fear I my talent misteuk,
   But what will ye hae of a fool.

recitative.

Poor Merry andrew, in the neuk,
    Sat guzzling wi' a Tinkler-hizzie;
They mind't na wha the chorus teuk,
    Between themsels they were sae busy:
At length wi' drink an' courting dizzy,
    He stoiter'd up an' made a face;
Then turn'd an' laid a smack on Grizzie,
    Syne tun'd his pipes wi' grave grimace.

Air.   Tune,   Auld Sir Symon.

Sir Wisdom's a fool when he's fou;
    Sir Knave is a fool in a Session,
He's there but a prentice, I trow,
    But I am a fool by profession.
My Grannie she bought me a beuk,
    An' I held awa to the school;
I fear I my talent misteuk,
    But what will ye hae of a fool.

29

For drink I would venture my neck;
    A hizzie's the half of my craft;
But what could ye other expect
    Of ane that's avowedly daft?

I ance was tied up like a stirk
    For civilly swearing and quaffing;
I, ance, was abus'd i' the kirk
    For towsing a lass i' my daffin.

Poor Andrew that tumbles for sport
    Let naebody name wi' a jeer:
There's ~~I'm~~ even, I'm tauld, i' the Court
    A Tumbler ca'd the Premier.

Observ'd ye yon reverend lad
    Mak faces to tickle the mob;
He rails at our mountebank squad,
    It's rivalship just i the job.

And now my conclusion I'll tell,
    For faith! I'm confoundedly dry;
The chiel that's a fool for himsel,
    Gude L—d, he's far dafter than I.

For drink I would venture my neck;
  A hizzie's the half of my Craft:
But what could ye other expect
  Of ane that's avowedly daft.
I, ance, was ty'd up like a stirk,
  For civilly swearing and quaffing;
I, ance, was abus'd i' the kirk,
  For towsing a lass i' my daffin.

Poor Andrew that tumbles for sport
  Let nae body name wi' a jeer;
There's even, I'm tauld, i' the Court
  A Tumbler ca'd the Premier.

Observ'd ye yon reverend lad
  Mak faces to tickle the Mob;
He rails at our mountebank squad,
  Its rivalship just i' the job.

And now my conclusion I'll tell,
  For faith I'm confoundedly dry:
The chiel that's a fool for himsel,
  Guid L—d, he's far dafter than I.

31

RECITATIVO—

Then neist outspak a raucle Carlin,
Wha kent fu' well to cleek the Sterlin';
For mony a pursie she had hooked,
An' had in mony a well been douked.
Her love had been a Highland laddie,
But weary fa' the waefu' woodie!
Wi' sighs an' sobs she thus began
To wail her braw John Highlandman—

Air   Tune.   O an' ye were dead Gudeman.—

A Highland lad my love was born,
The lalland laws he held in scorn,
But he still was faithfu' to his clan,
My galtant, braw John Highlandman.

        CHORUS—
        Sing hey my braw John Highlandman!
        Sing ho my braw John Highlandman!
        There's not a lad in a' the lan'
        Was match for my John Highlandman!

With his philabeg an' tartan plaid,
An' guid Claymore down by his side,
The ladies' hearts he did trepan,
My gallant, braw John Highlandman.
                Sing hey etc.

Recitativo ——

Then niest out spak a raucle Carlin,
Wha ken't fu' weel to cleek the Sterlin;
For mony a pursie she had hooked,
An had in mony a well been douked:
Her Dove had been a Highland laddie,
But weary fa' the waefu' woodie!
Wi' sighs an' sobs she thus began
To wail her braw John Highlandman.——

AIR.   Tune. O an' ye were dead Gudeman.——

A highland lad my Love was born,
The lalland laws he held in scorn:
But he still was faithfu' to his clan,
My gallant braw John Highlandman.
                Chorus ——
Sing hey my braw John Highlandman!
Sing ho my braw John Highlandman!
There's not a lad in a' the lan'
Was match for my John Highlandman.

With his philibeg, an' tartan plaid.
An' guid Claymore down by his side;
The ladies' hearts he did trepan,
My gallant braw John Highlandman.
                Sing hey &c.

33

We ranged a' from Tweed to Spey,
An' liv'd like lords and ladies gay:
For a lalland face he feared none,
My gallant, braw John Highlandman.
            Sing hey etc.

They banish'd him beyond the sea,
But ere the bud was on the tree,
Adown the cheeks the pearls ran,
Embracing my John Highlandman.
            Sing hey etc.

But, Och! they catch'd him at the last,
And bound him in a dungeon fast;
My curse upon them every one,
They've hang'd my braw John Highlandman.
            Sing hey etc.

And now a widow I must mourn
The pleasures that will ne'er return;
No comfort but a hearty can,
When I think on John Highlandman.
            Sing hey etc.

RECITATIVO.

A pygmy scraper wi' his fiddle,
Wha us'd to trystes an' fairs to driddle,
Her strappan limb an' gausy middle,
            He reach'd nae higher

We ranged a' from Tweed to Spey,
An' liv'd like lords an' ladies gay:
For a lalland face he feared none,
My gallant, braw John Highlandman.
          Sing hey &c.

They banish'd him beyond the sea,
But ere the bud was on the tree,
Adown my cheeks the pearls ran,
Embracing my John Highlandman.
          Sing hey &c.

But Och! they catch'd him at the last,
And bound him in a dungeon fast,
My curse upon them every one,
They've hang'd my braw John Highlandman
          Sing hey &c.

And now a Widow I must mourn
The Pleasures that will ne'er return;
No comfort but a hearty can,
When I think on John Highlandman.
          Sing hey &c.

          Recitativo —

A hungry feraher wi' his fiddle,
Wha aft to thriftes an' fairs to driddle,
Her flighan limb an' gaufy middle
          He reach'd nae higher

35

Had hol'd his heartie like a riddle,
    An' blawn't on fire.

Wi' hand on hainch, and upward e'e,
He croon'd his gamut, one, two, three,
Then in an *arioso* key,
        The wee Apollo,
Set off wi' *allegretto* glee
        His *giga* solo—

Air.   Tune, Whistle owre the lave o't

Let me ryke up to dight that tear,
An' go wi' me an' be my dear,
An' then your every care an' fear
    May whistle owre the lave o't.

CHORUS.
I am a Fiddler to my trade,
An' a' the tunes that e'er I play'd,
The sweetest still to wife or maid
    Was—Whistle owre the lave o't.

At kirns an' weddings we'se be there,
An' O, sae nicely's we will fare!
We'll bowse about till Dadie Care
    Sing, Whistle owre the lave o't.
                    I am etc.

Sae merrily's the banes we'll pyke,
An' sun oursels about the dyke;

Had hol'd his heartie like a riddle,
                    An' blawn 't on fire.

Wi' hand on hainch, and upward e'e,
He croon'd his gamut, one, two, three,
Then in an arioso key,
                    The wee Apollo
Set off wi' allegretto glee
                    His giga solo —

AIR. — Tune, Whistle owre the lave o't.

Let me ryke up to dight that tear,
An' go wi' me an' be my dear,
An' then your every care an' fear
          May whistle owre the lave o't.
          — Chorus —
     I am a Fiddler to my trade,
     An' a' the tunes that e'er I play'd,
     The sweetest still to wife or maid,
               Was whistle owre the lave o't.

At Kirns an' weddins we'se be there,
An' O sae nicely's we will fare!
We'll bowse about till Daddie Care
          Sing whistle owre the lave o't.
                    I am &c.
Sae merrily's the banes we'll pyke,
     An' sun oursells about the dyke;

An' at our leisure, when ye like
  We'll whistle owre the lave o't.
                    I am etc.

But bless me wi' your heav'n o' charms,
An' while I kittle hair on thairms,
Hunger, cauld, an' a' sic harms
  May whistle owre the lave o't.
                    I am etc.

RECITATIVO—

Her charms had struck a sturdy Caird
  As weel as poor gut-scraper;
He taks the Fiddler by the beard,
  An' draws a roosty rapier—
He swoor by a' was swearing worth
  To speet him like a pliver,
Unless he would from ~~this~~ that time forth
  Relinquish her for ever.

Wi' ghastly e'e, poor Tweedle Dee
  Upon his hunkers bended,
An' pray'd for grace wi' rueful face,
  An' so the quarrel ended.
But tho' his little heart did grieve
  When round the Tinkler prest her,
He feigned to snirtle in his sleeve
  When thus the Caird address'd her—

An' at our leisure when ye like
    We'll whistle owre the lave o't.
                I am &c.
But bless me wi' your heav'n o' charms,
An' while I kittle hair on thairms
Hunger, Cauld, an' a' sic harms
    May whistle owre the lave o't.
                I am &c.

        Recitativo —

Her charms had struck a sturdy Caird,
    As weel as poor Gutscraper;
He taks the Fiddler by the beard,
    An' draws a roosty rapier —
He swoor by a' was swearing worth
    To speet him like a Pliver,
Unless he would from that time forth
    Relinquish her for ever:
Wi' ghastly e'e poor Tweedledee
    Upon his hunkers bended,
An' pray'd for grace wi' ruefu' face,
    An' so the quarrel ended;
But tho' his little heart did grieve,
    When round the Tinkler prest her,
He feign'd to snirtle in his sleeve
    When thus the Caird address'd her —

39

Air.   Tune Clout the Caudron.—

My bonie lass, I work in brass,
    A Tinkler is my station;
I've travell'd round all Christian ground
    In this my occupation;
I've ta'en the gold, an' been enroll'd
    In many a noble squadron:
But vain they search'd, when off I march'd
    To go an' clout the Caudron.
                I've ta'en the gold,etc.

Despise that Shrimp, that wither'd imp,
    With a' his noise an' cap'rin,
An' take a share with those that bear
    The budget and the apron:
And *by* that stowp, my faith and houpe,
    And *by* that dear (X)Kilbagie,
If e'er you want, or meet with scant,
    May I ne'er weet my craigie!
                And by that stowp, etc.

(X)A peculiar sort of whiskie so called: a great favorite with
Poosie Nancie's Clubs.

AIR.   Tune, Clout the Caudron. ——

My bonie lass, I work in brass,
    A TINKLER is my station;
I've travell'd round all Christian ground
    In this my occupation;
I've ta'en the gold an' been enroll'd
    In many a noble squadron;
But vain they search'd when off I march'd
    To go an' clout the CAUDRON.
            I've ta'en the gold &c,

Despise that SHRIMP, that wither'd IMP,
    With a' his noise an' cap'rin;
An' take a share with those that bear
    The budget and the apron!
And by that STOWP! my faith an' houpe,
    And by that dear *Kilbaigie.
If e'er ye want, or meet with scant,
    May I ne'er Weet my craigie!
            And by that stowp, &c.

_____

    * A peculiar sort of Whiskie so called: a great
favorite with Poosie Nansie's Clubs. ——

RECITATIVO—

The Caird prevail'd—th' unblushing fair
  In his embraces sunk,
Partly wi' love, o'ercome sae sair,
  An' partly she was drunk.
Sir Violino, with an air
  That show'd a man o' spunk,
Wish'd unison between the pair,
An' made the bottle clunk
              To their health that night.

But hurchin Cupid shot a shaft
  That play'd a Dame a shavie;
The Fiddler rak'd, her fore and aft,
  Behint the Chicken cavie.
Her lord, a wight of Homer's(X) craft,
  Tho' limpan wi' the spavie,
He hirpl'd up, and lap like daft,
  And shor'd them *Dainty Davie*
              O' boot that night.

He was a care-defying blade
  As ever Bacchus listed!
Tho' Fortune sair upon him laid,
  His heart she ever miss'd it.

(X) Homer is allowed to be the eldest Ballad singer on record

Recitativo—

The Caird prevail'd— th'unblushing fair
    In his embraces sunk;
Partly wi' Love o'ercome sae fair,
    An' partly she was drunk:
Sir Violino with an air
    That show'd a man o'spunk,
Wish'd unison between the pair,
    An' made the bottle clunk
        To their health that night.

But hurchin Cupid shot a shaft,
    That play'd a Dame a shavie—
The Fiddler rak'd her, fore and aft,
    Behint the Chicken cavie:
Her lord, a wight of Homer's*craft,
    Tho limpan wi' the Spavie,
He hirpl'd up an' lap like daft,
    An' shor'd them Dainty Davie
        O' boot that night.

He was a care-defying blade
    As ever Bacchus listed!
Tho' Fortune fair upon him laid,
    His heart she ever miss'd it

Homer is allowed to be the eldest Ballad singer on
record

He had no wish but—to be glad,
  Nor want but—when he thristed;
He hated nought but—to be sad;
  An' thus the Muse suggested
                His sang that night:-

Air — Tune. for a' that an' a' that——

I am a Bard, of no regard
  Wi' gentle folks an' a' that;
But Homer like, the glowran byke,
  Frae town to town I draw that.

CHORUS—
For a' that, an' a' that,
  An' twice as muckle's a' that;
I've lost but ane, I've twa behin',
  I've wife eneugh for a' that.

I never drank the Muses' stank,
  Castalia's burn, an' a' that;
But there it streams, an' richly reams,
  My Helicon I ca' that.
                For a' that etc.

Great love I bear to all the Fair,
  Their humble slave an' a' that;
But lordly will, I hold it still
  A mortal sin to thraw that.
                For a' that etc.

He had no WISH but— to be glad,
    Nor WANT but— when he thristed:
He hated nought but— to be sad,
    An' thus the Muse suggested
        His sang that night.

Air —: Tune. for a' that an' a' that————

    I am a Bard of no regard,
        Wi' gentle folks an' a' that;
But HOMER like the glowran byke,
      Frae town to town I draw that.
      Chorus————
     For a' that an' a' that,
        An' twice as muckle's a' that;
I've lost but ane, I've twa behin',
      I've wife enough for a' that

    I never drank the Muses' STANK,
        Castalia's burn an' a' that,
But there it streams an' richly-reams,
     My Helicon I ca' that.
          For a' that &c.
Great love I bear to all the FAIR,
    Their humble slave an' a' that;
But lordly WILL, I hold it still
    A mortal sin to thraw that.
       For a' that &c.

In raptures sweet, this hour we meet,
  Wi' mutual love an' a' that:
But for how lang the flie may stang,
  Let Inclination law that.

                    For a' that etc.

Their tricks an' craft hae put me daft,
  They've taen me in, an' a' that;
But clear your decks, an' here's the SEX!
  I like the jads for a' that.

    For a' that, an' a' that,
      An' twice as muckle's a' that;
    My dearest bluid, to do them guid,
      They're welcome till't, for a' that.

RECITATIVO—

So sang the Bard—and Nansie's wa's
Shook with a thunder of applause
  Re-echoed from each mouth!
They toom'd their pocks, they pawn'd their duds,
They scarcely left to co'or their fuds
  To quench their lowan drouth;
Then owre again, the jovial thrang,
  The poet did request
To lowse his pack and wale a sang,
  A ballad o' the best.

In raptures sweet this hour we meet,
   Wi' mutual love an' a' that;
But for how lang the flie may stang,
   Let Inclination law that.
          For a' that &c.

Their tricks an' craft hae put me daft,
   They've taen me in, an' a' that;
But clear your decks an' here's the Sex!
   I like the jads for a' that.
     For a' that an' a' that
       An: twice as muckle's a' that;
My dearest bluid to do them guid,
    They're welcome till't for a' that.

Recitativo ——

So sung the Bard — and Nansie's waws
Shook with a thunder of applause
   Re-echo'd from each mouth!
They toom'd their pocks, they pawn'd their duds,
They scarcely left to cover their fuds,
   To quench their lowan drouth;
Then owre again the jovial thrang
   The Poet did request
To lowse his Pack an' wale a sang,
   A ballad o' the best.

47

He rising, rejoicing,
    Between his twa Deborahs,
Looks round him, an' found them
    Impatient for the chorus

Air — Jolly Mortals fill your glasses —

See the smoking bowl before us,
    Mark our jovial ragged ring!
Round and round take up the Chorus,
    And in raptures let us sing,—

CHORUS—
A fig for those by law protected!
Liberty's a glorious feast!
Courts for Cowards were erected,
Churches built to please the Priest!

What is title, what is treasure,
    What is reputations care?-
If we lead a life of pleasure,
'Tis no matter how or where!
                    A fig etc.

With the ready trick and fable
    Round we wander all the day;
And at night, in barn or stable
    Hug our doxies on the hay.
                    A fig etc.

He, rising, rejoicing,
   Between his twa *Deborahs*,
Looks round him an' found them
   Impatient for the Chorus

Air.— Tune, *Jolly Mortals fill your glasses* —

See the smoking bowl before us,
   Mark our jovial ragged ring !
Round and round take up the Chorus.
   And in raptures let us sing —
     Chorus——
    A fig for those by law protected !
    Liberty's a glorious feast !
   Courts for Cowards were erected,
    —Churches built to please the *Priest.*
What is title, what is treasure,
   What is reputation's care ?
If we lead a life of pleasure,
   'Tis no matter *HOW* or *WHERE.*
     A fig &c.
With the ready trick and fable
   Round we wander all the day ;
And at night, in barn or stable,
   Hug our doxies on the hay.
     A fig for &c.

49

Does the train-attended Carriage
  Thro' the country lighter rove?
Does the sober bed of Marriage
  Witness brighter scenes of love?
                A fig for etc.

Life is all a variorum,
  We regard not how it goes;
Let them cant about decorum,
  Who have character to lose.
                A fig for etc.

Here's to budgets, bags and wallets!
  Here's to all ~~our~~ the wandering train!
Here's our ragged Brats and Callets!
  One and all, cry out, AMEN!

A fig for those by law protected!
  Liberty's a glorious feast!
Courts for Cowards were erected,
  Churches built to please the priest.

Finis

Does the train-attended Carriage
   Thro' the country lighter rove?
Does the sober bed of Marriage
   Witness brighter scenes of love?
       A fig for &c.

Life is, all a variorum,
   We regard not how it goes;
Let them cant about decorum,
   Who have character to lose.
       A fig for &c.

Here's to budgets, bags and wallets!
   Here's to all the wandering train!
Here's our ragged Brats and Callets!
   One and all cry out, Amen!

A fig for those by law protected
   Liberty's a glorious feast!
Courts for Cowards were erected,
   Churches built to please the priest

    Finis

SONGS

FROM

THE JOLLY BEGGARS

Or

LOVE & LIBERTY

Illustrated by
John Hampson

The Soldier

John P. Hampson

I am a son of Mars, who have been in many wars,
And show my cuts and scars wherever I come;
This here was for a wench, and that other in a trench
When welcoming the French at the sound of the drum.
        Lal de daudle, Etc.

My prenticeship I past, where my leader breath'd his last,
When the bloody die was cast on the heights of Abram:
And I served out my trade, when the gallant game was play'd,
And the Moro low was laid at the sound of the drum.
        Lal de daudle, Etc.

I lastly was with Curtis, among the floating batt'ries
And there I left for witness an arm and a limb;
Yet let my country need me, with Elliot to head me,
I'd clatter on my stumps at the sound of a drum.

And now, tho' I must beg with a wooden arm and leg,
And many a tatter'd rag hanging over my bum,
I'm as happy with my wallet, my bottle and my callet,
As when I us'd in scarlet to follow a drum.

What tho', with hoary locks I must stand the winter shocks,
Beneath the woods and rocks oftentimes for a home!
When the tother bag I sell, and the tother bottle tell,
I could meet a troop of Hell at the sound of a drum!

Soldier's Woman

John P. Hampson

Air. *Tune, Sodger laddie*

I once was a maid tho' I cannot tell when,
And still my delight is in proper young men;
Some one of a troop of Dragoons was my dadie;
No wonder I'm fond of a Sodger laddie.
             Sing, Lal de Lal, Etc.

The first of my loves was a swaggering blade;
To rattle the thundering drum was his trade;
His leg was so tight and his cheek was so ruddy,
Transported I was with my Sodger laddie.

But the godly old Chaplain left him in the lurch;
The sword I forsook for the sake of the church;
He ventur'd the soul, and I risked the Body;
'Twas then I proved false to my Sodger laddie.

Full soon I grew sick of my sanctified Sot;
The regiment at large for a husband I got;
From the gilded Spontoon to the Fife I was ready;
I asked no more but a Sodger laddie.

But the Peace it reduc'd me to beg in despair,
Till I met my old boy in a Cunningham fair;
His rags regimental they flutter'd so gaudy;
My heart it rejoic'd at a Sodger laddy.

And now I have lived—I know not how long!
And still I can join in a cup and a song;
But whilst with both hands I can hold the glass steady,
Here's to thee, my Hero, my Sodger laddie.

Merry Andrew

John P. Hampson

Andante

Sir Wisdom's a fool when he's fou;
  Sir Knave is a fool in a Session,
He's there but a prentice I trow,
But I am a fool by profession.

My Grannie she bought me a beuk,
  An' I held awa to the School;
I fear I my talent misteuk,
  But what will ye hae of a fool.

For drink I would venture my neck;
  A hizzie's the half of my craft;
But what could ye other expect
  Of ane that's avowedly daft?

I ance was tied up like a stirk
  For civilly swearing and quaffing;
I, ance, was abus'd i' the kirk
  For towsing a lass i' my daffin.

Poor Andrew that tumbles for sport
  Let naebody name wi' a jeer:
There's I'm even, I'm tauld, i' the Court
  A Tumbler ca'd the Premier.

Observ'd ye yon reverend lad
  Mak faces to tickle the mob;
He rails at our mountebank squad,
  It's rivalship just i the job.

And now my conclusion I'll tell,
  For faith! I'm confoundedly dry;
The chiel that's a fool for himsel,
  Gude Lord, he's far dafter than I.

Old Woman

John P. Hampson

60

Brisk

CHORUS—

Sing hey my braw John Highlandman!
Sing ho my braw John Highlandman!
There's not a lad in a' the lan'
Was match for my John Highlandman!

A Highland lad my love was born,
The lalland laws he held in scorn,
But he still was faithfu' to his clan,
My gallant, braw John Highlandman.

With his philabeg an' tartan plaid,
An' guid Claymore down by his side,
The ladies' hearts he did trepan,
My gallant, braw John Highlandman.
        Sing hey etc.

We ranged a' from Tweed to Spey,
An' liv'd like lords and ladies gay:
For a lalland face he feared none,
My gallant, braw John Highlandman.
        Sing hey etc.

They banish'd him beyond the sea,
But ere the bud was on the tree,
Adown the cheeks the pearls ran,
Embracing my John Highlandman.
        Sing hey etc.

But, Och! they catch'd him at the last,
And bound him in a dungeon fast;
My curse upon them every one,
They've hang'd my braw John Highlandman.
        Sing hey etc.

And now a widow I must mourn
The pleasures that will ne'er return;
No comfort but a hearty can,
When I think on John Highlandman.
        Sing hey etc.

The Fiddler

John P. Hampson

Let me ryke up to dight that tear,
An' go wi' me an' be my dear,
An' then your every care an' fear
    May whistle owre the lave o't.

CHORUS.
I am a Fiddler to my trade,
An' a' the tunes that e'er I play'd,
The sweetest still to wife or maid
    Was—Whistle owre the lave o't.

At kirns an' weddings we'se be there,
An' O, sae nicely's we will fare!
We'll bowse about till Dadie Care
    Sing, *Whistle owre the lave o't.*
                    I am etc.

Sae merrily's the banes we'll pyke,
An' sun oursels about the dyke;
An' at our pleasure, when ye like
    We'll whistle owre the lave o't.
                    I am etc.

But bless me wi' your heav'n o' charms,
An' while I kittle hair on thairms,
Hunger, cauld, an' a' sic harms
    May whistle owre the lave o't.
                    I am etc.

The Tinker

Air. *Tune, Clout the Caudron*

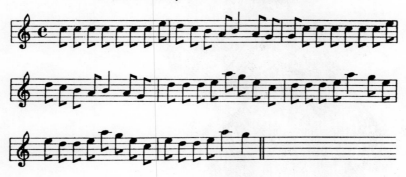

My bonie lass, I work in brass,
    A Tinkler is my station;
I've travell'd round all Christian ground
    In this my occupation;
I've ta'en the gold, an' been enroll'd
    In many a noble squadron:
But vain they search'd, when off I march'd
    To go an' clout the Caudron.
                    I've ta'en the gold, etc.

Despise that Shrimp, that wither'd imp,
    With a' his noise an' cap'rin,
An' take a share with those that bear
    The budget and the apron:
And *by* that stowp, my faith and houpe,
    And *by* that dear Kilbagie,
If e'er you want, or meet with scant,
    May I ne'er weet my craigie!
                    And by that stowp, etc.

John P. Hampson

The Poet

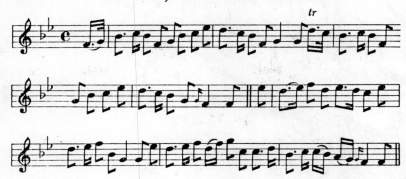

CHORUS—
For a' that, an' a' that,
  An' twice as muckle's a' that;
I've lost but ane, I've twa behin',
I've wife eneugh for a' that.

I am a Bard, of no regard
  Wi' gentle folks an' a' that;
But Homer like, the glowran byke,
  Frae town to town I draw that.

I never drank the Muses' stank,
  Castalia's burn, an' a' that;
But there it streams, an' richly reams,
  My Helicon I ca' that.
                    For a' that etc.

Great love I bear to all the Fair,
  Their humble slave an' a' that;
But lordly will, I hold it still
  A mortal sin to thraw that.
                    For a' that etc.

In raptures sweet, this hour we meet,
  Wi' mutual love an' a' that:
But for how lang the flie may stang,
  Let Inclination law that.

Their tricks an' craft hae put me daft,
  They've taen me in, an' a' that;
But clear your decks, an' here's the SEX
  I like the jads for a' that.

CHORUS
For a' that, an' a' that,
  An' twice as muckle's a' that;
My dearest bluid, to do them guid,
  They're welcome till't, for a' that.

THE POET'S
FINALE.

CHORUS—
A fig for those by law protected!
Liberty's a glorious feast!
Courts for Cowards were erected,
Churches built to please the Priest!

See the smoking bowl before us,
  Mark our jovial ragged ring!
Round and round take up the Chorus,
  And in raptures let us sing,—

What is title, what is treasure,
  What is reputations care?-
If we lead a life of pleasure,
  'Tis no matter how or where!
        A fig etc.

With the ready trick and fable
  Round we wander all the day;
And at night, in barn or stable
  Hug our doxies on the hay.
        A fig etc.

Does the train-attended Carriage
  Thro' the country lighter rove?
Does the sober bed of Marriage
  Witness brighter scenes of love?
        A fig etc.

Life is all a variorum,
  We regard not how it goes;
Let them cant about decorum,
  Who have character to lose.
        A fig etc.

Here's to budgets, bags and wallets!
  Here's to all our the wandering train!
Here's our ragged Brats and Callets!
  One and all, cry out, AMEN!

A fig for those by law protected!
Liberty's a glorious feast!
Courts for Cowards were erected,
Churches built to please the priest.

A NOTE ON THE SONGS

Robert Burns was not a musician, and yet he was responsible for perhaps the most brilliant outpouring of songs in all of our Western musical heritage.

He did learn to pick out a tune on the fiddle, and eventually to — as he put it — prick out a tune on paper. But obviously he had the most astonishing musical memory, in which were banked thousands of tunes, scraps of songs, titles and themes. Not all of them came from his mother and the farm servant of his childhood, from whom certainly he learned many — as he acknowledged. Many quite obviously came from a determined study of all the written sources he could find. He was what we would today term a 'lyric-writer'. And what lyrics he wrote!

Almost invariably he was able to select, from his vast mental store, the precise tune to fit a lyric. Alternatively, he was able to write words to fit whatever tune had caught his fancy.

Nowhere in the whole astonishing body of his work is this genius more clear than in *The Jolly Beggars*. Each lyric and each tune fit together into a seamless whole, and each is a delight. He did not write those tunes — although he was perfectly capable of taking some half-remembered scrap of tune and turning it into a song. In *The Jolly Beggars* he selected old and well-loved tunes, (many of them are still well-loved today), and wrote new words to them, or wrote original words if only the old tune existed.

Interestingly, some of the lyrics in *The Jolly Beggars* have a direct relationship with the old lyrics of the tunes he was using. For the Old Soldier's song *'I am a son of Mars'* he chose the tune *Soldier's Joy*. The Tinker's song *'My bonie lass, I work in brass'* uses the tune *Clout the Caudron*. The heart-stirring finale of *The Jolly Beggars*, *'See the smoking bowl before us'*, is fitted to the tune *Jolly mortals, fill your glasses*.

It is fascinating to speculate on how Burns approached his work when writing these songs. Did he have the tune in mind and write the lyric to fit? Was the lyric itself suggested by the words of the old song? Did he write the lyric in a particular metre then dredge his mind for a tune to fit? We shall never know the answers to those questions, and perhaps it is not important. A too-close analysis of a work of genius is usually a mistake. It can prevent full enjoyment and appreciation of the whole.

Nevertheless, it is interesting to see just where Burns got his tunes for *The Jolly Beggars*.

The Old Soldier's Song comes from the tune *Soldier's Joy*, which appears to have been printed for the first time in McGlashan's *Scots Measures,* 1781. Quite clearly, it is much older than that. It is a tune still popular, even if comparatively few know how Burns used it to set the scene for his Cantata.

The song of the Old Soldier's Woman has a very old tune that seems to have been printed for the first time in *Atkinson's M.S.,* 1694. It was reprinted many times in Scotland throughout the 18th. century, with various titles including *Northland Ladie*.

The Fool's song — *Sir Wisdom's a fool when he's fou* — uses the very old and very popular tune *Auld Sir Symon*. This was known in both England and Scotland as far back as Elizabethan times, when the English ballad *Ragged and torn* was sung to it. Over the many years, several different ballads, by unknown writers, were fitted to the tune, ballads of all kinds, but mostly drinking songs.

The tune of the Old Woman's Song — *A Highland lad my love was born* — also has a long and involved history, certainly going back at least to the Reformation. There is a parody of a popular song of the day, sung to this tune in *Gude and Godlie Ballads,* 1567. It was also popular through the years as a tune for dancing to.

The Tinker's song — *My bonie lass, I work in brass* — is to the tune of *Clout the Caudron*, and goes back to 1661, when it was printed in *Merry Drollery*. Of course it must be much older than that, since those were not original songs. *Merry Drollery* was printed in London in 1661, and the song was certainly English. It was 'scottified' by 1733, when it was printed in *Orpheus Caledonicus*.

The Finale — *See the smoking bowl before us* — uses the

tune *Jolly Mortals, fill your glasses!* It is an old English air, and appears to have been printed first in Ritson's *English Songs,* 1783.

Clearly, then, Burns cast his net very wide for the tunes he used so exquisitely in *The Jolly Beggars*. That he could do so demonstrates the breadth of his knowledge of song. That he did so, and fitted lyrics of such compelling power to those tunes, demonstrates again, if it be necessary, the scope of his particular genius.

It was by the use of popular tunes, the sort of tunes that might be whistled at work, that Burns ensured the popularity of *The Jolly Beggars*. It was by the use of such tunes, linked to his words of overwhelming power, that he ensured the immortality of *The Jolly Beggars* and of all the many songs he wrote.

THE JOLLY BEGGARS

or

LOVE & LIBERTY

A Cantata

by

Robert Burns

RECITATIVO.

When lyart leaves bestrow the yird,	*faded/earth*
Or, wavering like the bauckie-bird,	*bat*
Bedim cauld Boreas' blast;	
When hailstanes drive wi' bitter skyte,	*rebound*
And infant frosts begin to bite,	
In hoary cranreuch drest;	*hoar-frost*
Ae night at e'en a merry core	*one/evening/chorus*
O' randie, gangrel bodies	*disreputable/vagrant*
In Poosie Nansie's held the splore,	*debauch*
To drink their orra duddies:	*spare/clothes*
Wi' quaffing and laughing	
They ranted an' they sang,	
Wi' jumping an' thumping,	
The vera girdle rang.	*griddle*

First, niest the fire, in auld red rags   *next*
Ane sat; weel braced wi' mealy bags   *beggar's wallet for holding meal*
    And knapsack a' in order;
His doxy lay within his arm,   *woman*
Wi' usquebae and blankets warm   *whisky*
    She blinket on her sodger: *soldier*
An' ay he gies the tozie drab   *tipsy*
    The tither skelpin kiss,   *other/smacking*
While she held up her greedy gab   *mouth*
    Just like an aumous dish: *alms bowl*
        Ilk smack still, did crack still,
        Just like a cadger's whip,   *horse driver*
    Then staggering an' swaggering
    He roar'd this ditty up:-

THE OLD SOLDIER'S SONG

I am a son of Mars, who have been in many wars,
And show my cuts and scars wherever I come;
This here was for a wench, and that other in a trench
When welcoming the French at the sound of the drum.
            CHORUS. *Lal de daudle, Etc.*

My prenticeship I past, where my leader breath'd his last,
When the bloody die was cast on the heights of Abram:
And I served out my trade, when the gallant game was play'd,
And the Moro low was laid at the sound of the drum.   *Castle of El Moro, Santiago de*
                                                        Cuba, stormed in 1762

            CHORUS. *Lal de daudle, Etc.*

I lastly was with Curtis, among the floating batt'ries
And there I left for witness an arm and a limb;
Yet let my country need me, with Elliot to head me,
I'd clatter on my stumps at the sound of a drum.
            CHORUS. *Lal de daudle, Etc.*

And now, tho' ı must beg with a wooden arm and leg,
And many a tatter'd rag hanging over my bum,
I'm as happy with my wallet, my bottle and my callet,   *woman*
As when I us'd in scarlet to follow a drum.
            CHORUS. *Lal de daudle, Etc.*

What tho' with hoary locks I must stand the winter shocks,
Beneath the woods and rocks oftentimes for a home!
When the t'other bag I sell, and the t'other bottle tell,
I could meet a troop of hell at the sound of a drum!

RECITATIVO.

He ended; and the kebars sheuk   *rafters/shook*
   Aboon the chorus roar;
While frightened rattons backward leuk,   *rats/look*
   An seek the benmost bore: *inmost hole*
A fairy fiddler frae the neuk,   *from the corner*
   He skirl'd out, 'Encore!'   *shouted*
But up arose the martial chuck,
   An' laid the loud uproar:-

THE SONG OF THE OLD SOLDIER'S WOMAN

I once was a maid tho' I cannot tell when,
And still my delight is in proper young men;
Some one of a troop of Dragoons was my dadie;
No wonder I'm fond of a Sodger laddie.
         CHORUS. *Sing, Lal de Lal, Etc.*

The first of my loves was a swaggering blade;
To rattle the thundering drum was his trade;
His leg was so tight and his cheek was so ruddy,
Transported I was with my Sodger laddie.

But the godly old Chaplain left him in the lurch;
The sword I forsook for the sake of the church;
He ventur'd the soul, and I risked the Body;
'Twas then I proved false to my Sodger laddie.

Full soon I grew sick of my sanctified Sot;
The regiment at large for a husband I got;
From the gilded Spontoon to the Fife I was ready;   *officer's small halberd*
I asked no more but a Sodger laddie.

But the Peace it reduc'd me to beg in despair,
Till I met my old boy in a Cunningham fair;   *District of Ayrshire*
His rags regimental they flutter'd so gaudy;
My heart it rejoic'd at a Sodger laddy.

And now I have lived—I know not how long!
And still I can join in a cup and a song;
But whilst with both hands I can hold the glass steady,
Here's to thee, my Hero, my Sodger laddie.

RECITATIVO.

Poor Merry Andrew, in the neuk   *corner*
   Sat guzzling wi' a Tinkler-hizzie;   *drinking/tinker hussy*
They mind't na wha the chorus teuk,
   Between themsels they were sae busy:
At length wi' drink an' courting dizzy,
   He stoiter'd up an' made a face;   *staggered*
Then turn'd an' laid a smack on Grizzie,
   Syne tun'd his pipes wi' grave grimace:-   *soon*

THE FOOL'S SONG

Sir Wisdom's a fool when he's fou;
   Sir Knave is a fool in a Session,
He's there but a prentice I trow,
But I am a fool by profession.
My Grannie she bought me a beuk,   *book*
   An' I held awa to the school;
I fear I my talent misteuk,   *mistook*
   But what will ye hae of a fool?

For drink I would venture my neck;
   A hizzie's the half of my craft;
But what could ye other expect
   Of ane that's avowedly daft?

I ance was tied up like a stirk   *once/steer*
   For civilly swearing and quaffing;

I ance was abus'd i' the kirk
   For towsing a lass i' my daffin.   *ruffling/fooling*
Poor Andrew that tumbles for sport
   Let naebody name wi' a jeer:
There's even, I'm tauld, i' the Court
   A Tumbler ca'd the Premier.

Observ'd ye yon reverend lad
   Mak faces to tickle the mob;
He rails at our mountebank squad,—
   It's rivalship just i' the job!

And now my conclusion I'll tell,
   For faith! I'm confoundedly dry;
The chiel that's a fool for himsel,   *lad*
   Gude Lord! he's far dafter than I.

RECITATIVO.

Then neist outspak a raucle Carlin,   *next/strong & sturdy old woman*
Wha kent fu' well to cleek the Sterlin';   *snatch*
For mony a pursie she had hooked,
An' had in mony a well been douked.   *ducked*
Her love had been a Highland laddie,
But weary fa' the waefu' woodie!   *gallows*
Wi' sighs an' sobs she thus began
To wail her braw John Highlandman:-   *fine*

THE OLD WOMAN'S SONG

A Highland lad my love was born,
The lalland laws he held in scorn,   *lowland*
But he still was faithfu' to his clan,
My gallant, braw John Highlandman.

CHORUS.

     Sing hey my braw John Highlandman!
     Sing ho my braw John Highlandman!
     There's not a lad in a' the lan'
     Was match for my John Highlandman!

With his philabeg an' tartan plaid,   *kilt*
An' guid Claymore down by his side,   *great Highland sword*
The ladies' hearts he did trepan,   *seduce*
My gallant, braw John Highlandman.

We ranged a' from Tweed to Spey,
An' liv'd like lords and ladies gay;
For a lalland face he feared none,—
My gallant, braw John Highlandman.

They banish'd him beyond the sea,
But ere the bud was on the tree,
Adown the cheeks the pearls ran,
Embracing my John Highlandman.

But, Och! they catch'd him at the last,
And bound him in a dungeon fast;
My curse upon them every one—
They've hang'd my braw John Highlandman!

And now a widow I must mourn
The pleasures that will ne'er return;
No comfort but a hearty can,
When I think on John Highlandman.

RECITATIVO.

A pygmy scraper wi' his fiddle,
Wha us'd to trystes an' fairs to driddle,   *cattle markets/dawdle*
Her strappan limb an' gausy middle   *strapping/buxom*
      (He reach'd nae higher)
Had hol'd his heartie like a riddle,   *heart/sieve*
      An' blawn't on fire.   *blown it*

Wi' hand on hainch, and upward e'e,   *haunch/eye*
He croon'd his gamut, one, two, three,
Then in an *arioso* key,
      The wee Apollo,
Set off wi' *allegretto* glee
      His *giga* solo:-

THE FIDDLER'S SONG

Let me ryke up to dight that tear,   *reach/wipe*
 An' go wi' me an' be my dear,
An' then your every care an' fear
    May *whistle owre the lave o't.*   *the rest of it*

CHORUS.
I am a fiddler to my trade,
An' a' the tunes that e'er I play'd,
The sweetest still to wife or maid
Was—Whistle owre the lave o't.

At kirns an' weddings we'se be there,   *harvest homes*
An' O, sae nicely's we will fare!
We'll bowse about till Dadie Care   *booze*
    Sing, *Whistle owre the lave o't.*

Sae merrily's the banes we'll pyke,   *bones/pick*
An' sun oursels about the dyke;   *hedge*
An' at our leisure, when ye like
    We'll *whistle owre the lave o't.*

But bless me wi' your heav'n o' charms,
An' while I kittle hair on thairms,   *stir up/fiddle strings*
Hunger, cauld, an' a' sic harms   *all such*
    May *whistle owre the lave o't.*

RECITATIVO.

Her charms had struck a sturdy Caird   *tinker*
   As weel as poor gut-scraper;
He taks the Fiddler by the beard,
   An' draws a roosty rapier—   *rusty*
He swoor by a' was swearing worth
   To speet him like a pliver,   *spit/plover*
Unless he would from that time forth
   Relinquish her for ever.

Wi' ghastly e'e, poor Tweedle Dee
    Upon his hunkers bended,   *haunches*
An' pray'd for grace wi' rueful face,
    An' so the quarrel ended.
But tho' his little heart did grieve
    When round the Tinkler prest her,
He feigned to snirtle in his sleeve   *snigger*
    When thus the Caird address'd her:-

THE TINKER'S SONG

My bonie lass, I work in brass,
    A Tinkler is my station;   *tinker*
I've travell'd round all Christian ground
    In this my occupation;
I've ta'en the gold, an' been enroll'd
    In many a noble squadron:
But vain they search'd, when off I march'd
    To go an' clout the Caudron.   *mend/cauldron*
          I've ta'en the gold, etc.

Despise that Shrimp, that wither'd imp,
    With a' his noise an' cap'rin,
An' take a share with those that bear
    The budget and the apron: *wallet*
And *by* that stowp, my faith and houpe,   *pot/hope*
    And *by* that dear Kilbagie,   *Lowland malt whisky*
If e'er you want, or meet with scant,
    May I ne'er weet my craigie!   *wet my throat*
          And by that stowp, etc.

RECITATIVO.

The caird prevail'd—th' unblushing fair
    In his embraces sunk,
Partly wi' love, o'ercome sae sair,   *so sorely*
    An' partly she was drunk.

Sir Violino, with an air
    That show'd a man o' spunk,
Wish'd unison between the pair,
    An' made the bottle clunk
            To their health that night.

But hurchin Cupid shot a shaft
    That play'd a Dame a shavie;   *trick*
The Fiddler rak'd her fore and aft
    Behint the Chicken cavie.   *coop*
Her lord, a wight of Homer's craft,
    Tho' limpin wi' the spavie,   *spavin (horse disease)*
He hirpl'd up, and lap like daft,   *hobbled/leaped*
    And shor'd them *Dainty Davie*   *made a night of it*
            O' boot that night.

He was a care-defying blade
    As ever Bacchus listed!   *enlisted*
Tho' Fortune sair upon him laid,
    His heart she ever miss'd it.
He had no wish but—to be glad,
    Nor want but—when he thristed;   *thirsted*
He hated nought but—to be sad;
    An' thus the Muse suggested
            His sang that night:-

THE POET'S SONG

I am a Bard, of no regard
    Wi' gentle folks an' a' that;
But Homer-like, the glowran byke,   *staring crowd*
    Frae town to town I draw that.

CHORUS.
For a' that, an' a' that,
    An' twice as muckle's a' that;   *much*
I've lost but ane, I've twa behin',
    I've wife eneugh for a' that.

I never drank the Muses' stank,   *pond*
   Castalia's burn, an' a' that;
But there it streams, an' richly reams,   *foams*
   My Helicon I ca' that.

Great love I bear to all the fair,
   Their humble slave an' a' that;
But lordly will, I hold it still
   A mortal sin to thraw that.   *thwart*

In raptures sweet, this hour we meet,
   Wi' mutual love an' a' that:
But for how lang the flie may stang,   *sting*
   Let Inclination law that.   *determine*

Their tricks an' craft hae put me daft,
   They've taen me in, an' a' that;   *taken*
But clear your decks, an' here's 'THE SEX!'
   I like the jads for a' that.   *jades*

CHORUS
For a' that, an' a' that,
   An' twice as muckle's a' that;   *much*
My dearest bluid, to do them guid,   *blood/good*
   They're welcome till't, for a' that.   *to it*

RECITATIVO.

So sang the Bard — and Nansie's wa's   *walls*
Shook with a thunder of applause
   Re-echoed from each mouth!
They toom'd their pocks, they pawn'd their duds, *emptied their bags/clothes*
They scarcely left to co'or their fuds   *cover/backsides*
   To quench their lowan drouth: *burning thirst*
Then owre again, the jovial thrang,
   The Poet did request
To lowse his pack and wale a sang,   *loose/choose*
   A ballad o' the best.
   He rising, rejoicing,
      Between his twa Deborahs,
   Looks round him, an' found them
      Impatient for the chorus:-

THE POET'S FINALE

See the smoking bowl before us,
  Mark our jovial ragged ring!
Round and round take up the Chorus,
  And in raptures let us sing,—

CHORUS.
A fig for those by law protected!
Liberty's a glorious feast!
Courts for Cowards were erected,
Churches built to please the Priest!

What is title, what is treasure,
  What is reputation's care?-
If we lead a life of pleasure,
  'Tis no matter how or where!

With the ready trick and fable
  Round we wander all the day;
And at night, in barn or stable
  Hug our doxies on the hay.

Does the train-attended carriage
  Thro' the country lighter rove?
Does the sober bed of Marriage
  Witness brighter scenes of love?

Life is all a variorum,
  We regard not how it goes;
Let them cant about decorum,
  Who have character to lose.

Here's to budgets, bags and wallets!
  Here's to all the wandering train!
Here's our ragged Brats and Callets!
  One and all, cry out,—'AMEN'!

CHORUS
A fig for those by law protected!
  Liberty's a glorious feast!
Courts for Cowards were erected,
  Churches built to please the Priest!

Poetry, Politics and Forgetfulness

Whatever the image that springs to mind when the word 'poet' is mentioned, it is worth recalling Auden's dictum that a poet only feels himself to be such when he is finishing the last draft of a poem.   In between these high spots, the poet lives his ordinary life, and unless he is one of the fortunate few who make a living by writing, he has to earn his living elsewhere — perhaps as a teacher, librarian, farmer, lawyer or exciseman.   When Burns wrote *The Jolly Beggaars* he did it as a poet, and a great one.   When he wrote to George Thomson that he had '.....forgot the Cantata you allude to as I kept no copy and did not know that it was in existence.....' he was a man with a living to earn as an officer of Excise in His Hanoverian Majesty's Service.

We may either accept the poet's statement, or regard it as hardly more credible than Sam Coleridge's convenient visitor from Porlock.   If we think that poet Burns remembered the Cantata well enough, we must consider gauger Burns's reason for feigning amnesia. It is significant that a few months before the letter to Thomson, Robert Burns had been the subject of an Inquiry by the Excise Board into his loyalty to a Hanoverian establishment who were his ultimate employers.   Up to this point in his life, Burns was a man whose only success was his poetry, and then only as regards literary reputation; financially his poetry was as much dogged by ill luck as most of his other enterprises. The excise post was the last chance for Burns and his dependants to enjoy a modest degree of security, and this was in jeopardy.   Had the Board good reason for such an Inquiry?

Robert Burns had professed himself to be a Jacobite, and on the outbreak of the French Revolution, a Jacobin.

It is wrong to see the Jacobite attachment in Scotland as a struggle of Roman Catholic Stuart against Protestant Hanoverian. The movers behind the Forty-Five Rising were not Roman Catholics, but Scottish Episcopalians. After its failure, Butcher Cumberland burned down the Episcopalian chapels and arrested a number of Episcopalian clergy. One of them, who had taken no part in any battle, was executed. Those whose ancestors had written provisos against royal tyranny into the Declaration of Arbroath were unlikely to have much sympathy with Stuart claims to Divine Right, but they had a great deal of sympathy towards the idea of Scottish independence. An English spy, Daniel Defoe, wrote of the Scots at the time of the dissolution of their Parliament in 1707 that he had never seen a people so angry. There were three revolts in Scotland in under forty years from that date, the last of which, before its disastrous defeat at Culloden in 1746, had almost frightened the life out of the Hanoverian succession. One of the common slogans of the Jacobite army was *Alba is gun Aonaidh!* (Scotland and no Union!), and the most famous of Jacobite poets, the highly educated Alasdair Macdonald, wrote two bitter lines at the end of a poem about that ill-starred uprising which may be translated:

> Are you not ashamed of yourself, poor sad Scotland to have left a handful of Gaels in the breast of battle?

It was with this kind of Jacobitism that many Scots (Robert Burns included), no matter what their sects, had great sympathy. Burns had claimed to be of Jacobite stock, wrote letters to that effect, produced Jacobite songs, and drank Jacobite toasts. It is totally beside the point to say that Gilbert would have none of his brother's Jacobite pretensions. It is what *Robert* Burns said that is important. Had he said it fifty years earlier, Gilbert's denials would not have saved his brother from arrest. Of course, it had by then become safe to be a parlour Jacobite, but it was hardly a cautious attitude in one who worked for a Hanoverian administration. It is also noteworthy that Ramsay and Fergusson, whom Burns much admired, had Jacobite leanings.

Much more serious were Burns's sympathies with the French Revolution (as with the American Revolutionaries) in whose cause he had been been a little more active. He had sent a consignment of carronades to help them in their struggle, and these were said to have been seized at Dover together with the message of goodwill which accompanied them. It is unlikely that the authorities did not know of this, although the Revolution had been fashionable with all sorts and conditions in those early days. He was also given to making supportive speeches in public and writing tactless letters to unlikely sympathisers, after the early popularity of the Revolution had begun to wane.

Findlater, Burns's superior officer in the Excise at Dumfries, gave him an exemplary character in his report, and it is not beyond belief that he gave a word or two of worldly advice to Robin, whose political discretion was hardly in the same class as his poetry. At any rate, prudence may have been the reason behind the letter to Thomson: he just wanted to forget the Cantata, with its defiant John Highlandman and anarchic beggars. Perhaps the fact that *Scots Wha Hae* was published anonymously lends force to this view. Another writer of low-life musical works, John Gay, got away with his *Beggar's Opera,* but its sequel, *Polly,* was suppressed by the influence of a government stung by its satire. Did Burns know this?

There is a second possibility. Burns had wanted to include *The Jolly Beggars* in a previous collection, but had been advised against it by the Reverend Hugh Blair, Professor of Belles Lettres. It was, said Blair, '...*much too licentious.'* Burns at this time was trying to further his literary career, and he may have thought it would give offence to just those people whose critical approval he sought. Of course, the Cantata had great success on its posthumous publication, but Burns may have been unsure of its reception. He was none too good at gauging the reactions of the gentry, as his unfortunate solecism at Friar's Carse indicates, and his alienation of Mrs. Dunlop underlines.

But we must also consider the possibility that he was quite honest in his claim of forgetfulness. The years between the writing of the Cantata and the letter to Thomson had been hectic in more ways than one. He may himself not have known just how good it was, for in my view (contrary to what Tom Atkinson claims in his Introduction to this present volume) poets are often not the best judges of their own work. The mass of dreadful verse published by great poets lends support to my view. Should anyone doubt this critical blindness, let us recall the case of Goldsmith, in trouble for debt. He was rescued by Samuel Johnson who found that the improvident Irishman had a manuscript in his cupboard. Johnson read it, took the manuscript round to a printer and obtained the means of rescuing Goldsmith from his predicament. The manuscript was *The Vicar of Wakefield* which had been completed some years before. Plainly, Goldsmith's opinion of his work was much lower than that of Johnson or the printer. If Burns, like Goldsmith, had come to underestimate his Cantata, it is not unlikely that the events of the preceding years had pushed it to the bottom of his mind.

Fortunately for us, however, the Cantata was not entirely forgotten. It was published in 1799 by Stewart and Meikle in Glasgow and was an immediate success; a work which some consider to be Robert Burns's finest production.

It is said that the 'trigger' for *The Jolly Beggars* was a visit to Poosie Nancies dive in Mauchline, and there seems no good reason why we should doubt James Smith's later account of it. The idea of drama and song about low life was not new. Fletcher's *Beggar's Bush*, and John Gay's *Beggar's Opera* were by no means alone as antecedents of Burns's work. But Burns transformed his memory of the ragged band into a great creation in the fire of what Thomas Carlyle, in a piece which praised *Love and Liberty* as superior to both Fletcher and Gay, called his 'poetic vigour.' One of the reasons why the Cantata works so well lies in Lockhart's shrewd contrast of Burns and Crabbe, in which he points out that Crabbe was writing from above, whereas Burns was writing from within the group. Not only is he within the group, he is speaking from behind the masks of his characters, in varying degrees of intensity.

It is not easy for a writer to distance himself totally from his created figures. They may well turn out to be *personae* no matter whether they speak his sympathies or his antipathies, and in *The Jolly Beggars* it is Burns's viewpoint that most of them take. There is a certain school of poetical commentators today who seem to think that poetry should not express a viewpoint, political, religious, social or anything else, but the history of the art is not on their side. Burns, as well as most of his readers, would have found such a standpoint laughable. The lively opinions of major poets come strongly through their collected works, and no intelligent reader of Burns can have much doubt as to his attitudes.

Another characteristic of Burns's work is his fondness for difficult stanza forms and clarity of expression. It has been rightly remarked that this is a very Celtic attribute. There is an early Gaelic verse of four lines and twenty four words in which all four lines are tightly tied together by classic conventions which link twelve of the words by some bardic device, and still manage to make crystal clear sense at the end of it all, for as Coleridge remarked, poetry must be more than good sense, but it dare not be less.

It is a great pity that those who write about Scottish poetry do not try to read modern Scottish linguistic scholarship. Those who comment on Burns's apparent Celtic attributes almost always launch out into an attempt to claim some rather remote Highland ancestry for him. Robert Burns's father was a man of the Mearns, not a Gaelic-speaking Highlander. It does not seem to strike such commentators that Robert Burns was born into an area which, at the time of his birth, was very Scottish indeed; which had produced the two chief founders of Scottish freedom from English domination, William Wallace and Robert Bruce; where in 1560 the people of Burns's native Carrick had been described as being for the most part Gaelic speaking; wherein, a few miles from Burns's own birthplace, Walter Kennedy lived, who defended his native Gaelic speech in the *flyting* with William Dunbar, and at the same time, not far away, Alexander Montgomerie was writing macaronic poetry in Gaelic and Scots.

Burns was born in 1759, and it is claimed that the last speaker of Ayrshire Gaelic, Margaret MacMurray, died within a few miles of Burns's birthplace in 1760. It was not from any remote Argyllshire ancestor that Burns heard the old stories so dear to the Gael: it was from his Carrick mother, Agnes Brown and the old Carrick woman Betty Davidson.

Gaelic had been the tongue of Ayrshire and the south-west for a thousand years, and before that the language was of the other Celtic group. Modern linguistic experts disagree about the *terminus ad quem* of Gaelic in Carrick, but most would say, round about 1700. (See J. MacQueen: *The Gaelic Speakers of Galloway and Carrick*. Scottish Studies Vol.17. Part

One). The Scots dialect of Galloway and Carrick is richly peppered with words of Gaelic origin (see MacTaggart's *Gallovidian Encylopedia*) and a notable Galloway historian was attending the *tigh-fhaire* in Protestant Galloway at the end of the 19th century (McKerlie). Burns himself makes us aware that he knew this was the kingdom of the Celtic king Coel. In an area where the names of farms, hills and villages are predominantly in a Gaelic which is readily understood by any *modern* speaker of the language, there is no need to worry about Burns's Celtic ambience; it surrounded him in his youth, every bit as much as in any modern Highland village where Gaelic has become a mere memory. Modern attempts to carve Scotland up do not stand the historical test in language, culture or national attitudes.

Those, then, who see the Celtic influence in the complicated patterns and clear outlines of the Cantata (rather than in the half dozen or so Gaelic words therein) do not need to go gene-hunting in Lorne to establish Robert Burns's Celtic *bona-fides*.

The Recitativo and some of the songs have a high Scots lexis. Some songs are in standard English, and others have a Scottish flavour imparted to them by the use of a few words and turns of phrase. One often hears the question 'Why did he not do it all in Scots?' This is most often asked by those whose ear is familiar with Scots. To those for whom Scots is a first tongue, Scots poetry has an impact on them that, all other things being equal, English cannot have. It should be considered, however, that anyone other than a Scot of this dying breed may get just as much, if not more, from a poem that is less full of Scots words which he imperfectly understands. The idea that Burns meant to depict the soldier and his woman as English hardly seems valid.

In writing some of the songs in English, Burns may have had an idea beyond mere variety. Burns was a man who had read widely; he was highly articulate in standard English, both in verse and prose, and it is said (and it is highly likely) that he could speak better English than many of the Edinburgh gentry who attempted without success to patronise him. In Scotland today, it is often an educated Scot, using standard English for his professional transactions, who possesses the most extensive vocabulary of Gaelic or Scots.

Burns was in fact caught in the Scottish Writers' Predicament (discussed at length in *Chapman 35/36*). He knew his strength lay in poetry; he wished to be a distinctly Scottish as opposed to an English (or at any rate 'North British') poet, but felt that to write only in Scots would deprive him of that extensive audience which his talent certainly deserved. One has only to consider the fate of the splendid Gaelic poets of our own time to see the point. There were attempts to dissuade him from writing in Scots, but he had the integrity to resist them:. to put his own native truth before the attractions of the market place.

The stanza of the initial Recitativo is that of *The Cherry and the Slae* by Alexander Montgomerie, another Ayrshire poet, and one skilled in Gaelic. It is worth pointing out here that literary commentators, baffled by Montgomerie's title of *The Highland Captain* need look no further than Dunbar's description of Kennedy to discover that in those days the south-west of Scotland was referred to as 'helant'. Burns had read Montgomerie's poems and used this stanza form with great skill both in Scots and English. In the Cantata it is used to paint the approaching winter in a few short eloquent lines. We can hear the wind that rustles the leaves, feel *cauld Boreas' blast* (a man may write in Scots and know the Greeks, said Burns: this is an old and noble tongue, not the speech of boors). The *hailstanes* that *skyte* on Scottish lugs are made harder by the long flat vowels of the first word and the Norse consonants of the second; hailstones that bounce do so in gentler climes. We are thoroughly chilled in the first few lines, before being invited into the contrasting comfort of a room which is a bit like the haggis: warm, reeking and in its own way rich. Like those at the top, those at the bottom of the heap can enjoy the creature comforts at their own level. The soldier, scarred, crippled and discarded when of no further use is by no means downhearted. A vestige of former discipline remains to mark him off from the others: his knapsack is *a' in order*. His doxy's *greedy gab.....like an aumous dish* is a fitting simile in verse about beggars.

The Old Soldier's Song has end rhyme and internal rhyme, and although Burns may not have known it, an endstopping word which rhymes with a word in the middle of the next line is a Gaelic prosodic device called *aicill*. Of course, the stanza could have been written to put all the rhymes at the end, but that is not the way it is done, and it is a very complicated form. English is not rich in rhyme, but Burns sustains the demanding rhyme-scheme without a hint of bathos.

No matter how you try to read the lines, the timing sounds like a systematic drum solo. The suggestion that the English of the song hints at the soldier's background seems very thin. On the Heights of Abraham the private soldiers' language was more likely to be Gaelic. There were very few soldiers, even in the ranks of English regiments who spoke the standard English of the poem. Burns seeks variety, and at the same time means to show, with undoubted success, that he can produce a fine song in standard English. In any case, he is writing a 'musical', not striving for a literal, 'kitchen sink' realism. The shaking *kebars* show that the song was well received, and we are introduced to the undersized musician for the first time as the old soldier's woman comes forward to sing, a boldness that is in character: it was her man who earned the *Encore!*

The Song of the Old Soldier's Woman is also fitted to a drum-like metre, this time with a brisk dancing swagger which suits the nature of the woman, whose attitude is that of the boozy, devil-may-care who has seen better days. Burns had noticed, long before Shaw, that it is only those at the very bottom or the very top of society who are capable of this total abandonment of 'respectable' attitudes. This is a 'daughter of the regiment' of opposite polarity to the colonel's lady; whatever view one takes of her sexual *mores*, her military loyalty is impeccable. Burns gets in another anti-clerical jab here in his line on the chaplain. One can imagine the Reverend Hugh Blair's attitude to this, but a man of his literary background can hardly have failed to appreciate the poetic excellence of the line:

From the gilded Spontoon to the Fife I was ready.
no matter what his views might be on the subject of chastity. The spontoon and the fife, linked by their obvious phallic connotations, are at either end of the the military spectrum. The decorated and shining halberd, a symbol of commissioned rank, is indicative of the officer's finery, the more expensive regimentals; the fife, possibly played by a band-boy, is small and shrill, but not without a few shining appurtenances. The final word of the line is a terse but powerful expression of the lady's happy promiscuity. Her present man has even

less status than the fifer, but he is far from being a mere shadow. She finds his familiar military background a comfort, and loves the flutter of his tattered red coat. Note also that she needs two hands to hold a glass steady; she and her man are not just casualties of war, but of peace as well. There is a backbone of social comment behind the easy gaiety of the song.

The Merry Andrew's Song lacks the fire and brilliance of the two songs which precede it. The redoubtable Aberdonian Jamie Fleeman was once asked by a very superior gentleman 'Are you the Laird of Udny's fool?' and replied 'Aye. An' whase fool are you?' The 'simple' Jamie seems to have encompassed the theme of this song more succinctly than Burns. It does not stand a chance, sandwiched as it is between two excellent pieces, but we cannot blame Burns for its selection. Perhaps it is there because its slow, rather sad tune supplies a contrast. A few of the poet's own resentments are expressed by the Merry Andrew. If the Cantata was first drafted in 1785, it is significant that it was also the year when Burns himself had been 'abus'd i' the Kirk' for his affair with Elizabeth Paton.

The song of the sturdy, thieving Old Woman is one of sheer defiance. It is a fine, rousing song which is sometimes sung to a tune with the fitting title of *The White Cockade*, for the sentiment of this song, for all that our cateran does not go beyond Tweed, is Jacobite. 'Lalland laws' were Hanoverian, and had forbidden the wearing of 'tartan, plaid or any part of the Highland garb' or the carrying of 'any gun, sword, pistol or arm whatever' between 1747 and 1757, two years before the poet's birth. The old woman's champion is not merely defying the ordinary laws against robbery, he is defying those laws expressly designed to extinguish the Gaelic identity. Nor does Burns miss the aristocratic attitudes of the Gael, for the pair live 'like lords and ladies gay', an ironic contrast to the present condition of the singer. This song might not have gone down too well in a Hanoverian-administered Excise Board, for the comic visit of the fourth George to Edinburgh in full Highland garb was many years ahead.

The following *recitativo* is written in a stanza form called 'Standard Habbie' after a poem made to one Habbie Simpson, piper of Kilbarchan, by Sir Robert Sempill of Beltrees, although the form has an older ancestry. Nowadays it is often called the 'Burns

Stanza' from Burns's extensive use of it. Burns was not given to experiment with verse form; he preferred to use old forms to write new poems.

Though Burns was an expert at fitting words to a tune, he was modest enough about his formal musical education, but he seems to have studied it in some small degree, as the musical terms indicate. 'Apollo', like 'Boreas', is dropped into a Scots context, and the small musician has no mean opinion of his abilities to entertain, while the chorus is a reference to his sexual expertise. The tripping dance of the tune to which the words are set is appropriate to the 'kirns' and 'weddings' at which he assures his love they will be welcome. There is an air of genteel courtesy about his wooing which is roughly brushed aside by the bullying caird, whose sanguinary threat to 'spleet him like a pliver' ridicules the poor fiddler's tender body and lack of inches. The 'roostiness' of the rapier adds a gruesome overtone to the 'pliver' image. The fiddler begs for mercy and salves his pride by 'snirtling in his sleeve' at the coarse directness of the tinker's approach. The tinker has a philistine contempt for the fiddler's music. Food, drink and sex are his concerns, says he. We tend to forget that this is exactly what the fiddler said, for all his airs and graces: he gets with his fiddle what the caird gets with his hammer. The mender of pots and pans gives us a song which could be sung while 'clouting the caudron', and again there is a proliferation of end rhymes and internal rhymes. This song has a distinctly Scottish flavour, but the sprinkling of Scots words is fairly light. Why this light sprinkling of Scottish lexis? One of the reasons is that the rhymes would not work so well if it were wholly in Scots. Burns and many other Scots poets sometimes 'cheat' when a standard English rhyme makes a better agreement; the use of only a scattering of Scots opens the door to a wider supply of rhymes. In Ayrshire Scots, the first three lines of the Caird's song would be:-

My bonie *lass,* I wark in *bress*
a tinkler is my station,
I've trevellt *roon* aw Christian *grunn*......

The loss of agreement in the rhymes is obvious. Conversely, *stowp* and *houpe* make a better rhyme than standard English *stoup* and *hope*. *Gold* and *enrolled* cannot be replaced by *gowd* and *enrow'd* (like *ow* in cow) because Scots do not *enrow*, they *list* (as appears later in the Recitativo).

The tinker, despite his lack of courtly manners, gets his way, and the fiddler finds solace in another lady. We are told that he

.....raked her fore and aft
Behint the chicken cavie.

What would the prim Mrs. Riddel make of that, one wonders, and perhaps Robin wondered too. Cupid, Homer and Bacchus appear in the heavily Scots Recitativo; it is quite noticeable that the classical references appear in the most heavily Scots areas of the Cantata. Castalia, Helicon and the Muses are found in the very Scots *Poet's Song* and not in the standard English *Poet's Finale*. The modern metropolitan affectation that the sliding diphthongs and intrusive liaisons of Cockney variants of English are the only reputable way to speak that language, and the attitude that there are no other languages on the island despite the persistence of Welsh, Gaelic and Scots, is an irritant to many educated people outside that Pale in our own day.

Burns was irritated by precisely the same assumptions. He is making the point that Scots is not a language of provincial dunces, and that it is not the many-tongued Scot who is parochial, but his linguistic detractors. Why else should he bother to interpose sections of standard English verse in *Tam O' Shanter*? It is absurd to assume that he could not have written it all in Scots (and might well have preferred to); those who do not think that he was demonstrating his ability in *their* language as well as his own are obliged to supply another reason for the poet's linguistic choices.

The *Poet's Song* is no mask, but naked Burns. It is the verse of a man who knows his talent and is exasperated by his lack of recognition. He is a Bard

.....of no regard
wi gentle folks an' a' that.

In 1793, at the time of the letter to Thomson, that was no longer true, but the Cantata was written *before* the Kilmarnock Edition. It is sometimes said that his slighting references to *the Muses' stank, Castalia's burn* and *Helicon* are a complaint about his lack of learning. But if all those who cannot, or have forgotten how to, read the Greek and Latin classics in the original tongues are to be classified as unlearned, then there are very few learned people in the world. Despite his little Latin and less Greek, it would be a bold person who called Shakespeare 'unlearned'. It is much more likely that Burns is emphasising a point that he has already made excellently well —that beggars are as good a subject for poetry as any other, that poetry written by ordinary men about the ragged underdog is better stuff than the classical maundering of poetasters.

The profligate duke's song in *Rigoletto* (written seventy years later), might almost be a paraphrase of this Poet's Song, and were it not that the characters are tatterdemalions rather than noblemen; the Poet's Finale sounds as if it had been written as an anthem for the Abbey of Thelema (or perhaps Medmenham).

Remember Gauger Burns, emerging from the Inquiry with a sigh of relief; perhaps he has had a hint of future promotion if he keeps his nose clean. Think of him picking up a letter of enquiry from the egregious Thomson; consider how he might have reflected on the Cantata, and put yourself in his shoes.

> A fig for those by law protected!
> Liberty's a glorious feast!
> Courts for cowards were erected,
> Churches built to please the Priest!

Well, perhaps so. But a man has a living to earn, and poetry will scarcely provide enough for Jean and the bairns. Yon Inquiry was a kittle business. Better not have Thomson stirring up a wasps' byke again. Feign ignorance.

Let us give thanks, however, that *Love and Liberty* survived.

William Neill

The Blew Blanket Library

The *Blew* (or Blue) *Blanket* was the privileged insignia of the craftsmen of Edinburgh in the time of James III. It was pledged to them by Privy Seal in 1482 when the craftsmen of the city, together with the Merchants and other loyal subjects, marched on Edinburgh Castle and freed their King. It remained their insignia for centuries, and one of the original Blew Blankets is today in the Museum of Antiquities in Edinburgh.

The *Blew Blanket Library* is a collection of new books on Scotland by Scottish writers. Its aim is to provide a forum where writer-craftsmen of all types can display their goods in the context of Scotland today.

Published with this Volume
in
The Blew Blanket Library

Tall Tales From An Island
Peter Macnab

An intriguing medley of Tales from Mull — although they could equally well have come from any one of the Hebrides or anywhere in the Highlands. Witches and Warlocks, lovers and liars, heroes and headless horsemen all roar through these stories, which Peter Macnab learned round the ceilidh-fires of his childhood. He re-tells them now in prose rich with the rythms of the Hebrides, and shot through with strong love and deep compassion.

ISBN 0 946487 07 3   Price £3:95

The Crofting Years
Francis Thompson

A deeply researched social history of crofting in the Highlands and Islands. In its short lifetime of one hundred years, the crofting system of landholding has had profound effects upon Scotland and the Scots. Francis Thompson, a Gaelic scholar of high repute, who lives in Stornoway, has written of crofting with intimate knowledge. His vivid descriptions of crofting life in the past and now are essential for understanding modern Scotland. This book is no exercise in nostalgia for a dead past, but with restrained passion and pity, Francis Thompson takes us into the homes and the very minds of those who fought so desperately for security on their land. And he looks at, and fears for, the future. Francis Thompson has not produced a dull book of history, but a chronicle, beautifully written, of a way of life.

ISBN 0 946487 06 5   Price £3:00

The Edge Of The Wood
Alan Bold

This is Alan Bold's first solo collection of short stories, and it is an impressive one. Alan Bold himself claims that much of the inspiration for the stories comes from the kind of gossip with which Scotland is so enriched. It may be gossip, but it has passed through the pen of a master-craftsman. We have come to expect this of Alan Bold, but here his vision has run free — so we have tales of the Scottish reality of today, tales which well withstand comparison with the masters of the Scottish short story, in whose ranks Alan Bold can now stand.

It is a fine collection, ranging from murder in a Scottish village to a Black Hole in Space, from a man's love for his dog to a young poet's first love and first poem.

ISBN 0 946487 08 1   Price £4:25

Coming soon from The Blew Blanket Library:
New Poems by William Neill.

This collection of new poems by William Neill is an important addition to the body of Scottish poetry. Writing in the three languages of his country, and translating between them all, William Neill expresses a controversial view of Scotland today in lyrical work of extraordinary power.

Published By
LUATH PRESS,
Barr, Ayrshire.